QUICK AS
SHADOWS
PASSING

For Vern —
an authority on
these matters.
Best wishes!
C.M. Guneuielle

9/21/95

Also by C. W. Gusewelle

A Paris Notebook
An Africa Notebook

QUICK AS SHADOWS PASSING

by
C.W. GUSEWELLE

The Westphalia Press

The Dohman-Boessen House
Loose Creek, Missouri 65054

1988

Cover design by Dorothy Day
Back cover photograph by Loeb Granoff

Library of Congress Cataloging-in-Publication Data

Gusewelle, C. W. (Charles W.)
Quick as shadows passing.

I. Title.
AC8.G978   1988   081

ISBN 0-915637-09-X

88-28069

ACKNOWLEDGMENT

These bits of lives first appeared in
The Kansas City Star.

For children smooth
and furred

The House Lion

*When he was new in this world, and had no
wisdom, a blown leaf in the park was his
mortal enemy.*

*For the first six years he had one apartment
window of sun. And waited warm on the sill
through the silent afternoons of his mistress's
working bachelorhood.*

The darting birds, too, alarmed him.

*The second six years he prowled the larger
kingdom of a house—shared it with a heavy-
footed man, the man's three dogs, two
creeping infants in their time. Survived the
barkings-at and the intemperate huggings.
Dispensed justice with a paw whose claws he
kept sheathed. Mastered them all.*

*Caught a basement mouse, once. Brought it
up in the morning to display. Then, not
knowing how to kill it—or maybe why to kill
it—let it get away. His one trophy.*

*Grew old, more patient. Let dogs and
children touch noses with him. Slept a lot.*

*Watched the new cat come, a shaggy
fugitive from the homeless cold of winter—and
must have read in that the first sign of things
ending. Others beginning. But made his peace*

yet again. Slipped away one whole night with
that new cat, that outdoor cat. Saw things
he'd never dreamed of, and came back
smelling of the jungle, eyes narrowed to slits
of ancient triumph.

Moved slower now. Slept more. Remembered
it all—the leaf, the darting birds, his mouse,
that stolen night. Was full of years.

Lay down at last on a friendly rug.

Did not wake up.

Still prowls sometimes, at the eye's corner,
in a certain fall of sunlight in an empty room.

Contents

I.

1. The Short Morning

Time, stand still.

Stop just here, just now—on this cool, green morning, with the early sun pale through new leaves and my small garden flourishing and the children awake in their room and the gray kitten, Roosevelt, marching along the top of the board fence.

My daughters have had a little friend to spend the night. Theirs is a wonderful and peculiar age. An age it will be painful to watch them leave. They are at the very threshold of much, and yet are childish still. A part of their lives does not include us any more, but only a part. And it is, for a little while longer, a bearable fraction.

They have wakened early with their friend. The three voices, light and melodic, come down from an upper window to where I sit here, walled in by greenery, watching the day begin. I cannot hear what they are saying, nor is it proper that I should. Their concerns, at this hour, are their own. They are entitled to have secrets. But I do hear the general tone of the talk, which contains a kind of contentment that has to do with more than their just having crept from bed. They are full already of the inexpressible languor of summer coming on.

Who does not remember that feeling? There is victory in it—the anticipation of pure and perfect release. No segment of a life to be found later will ever unfold with a riper, more pungent hedonism than a child's summer. In the last days of school, as freedom nears, a kind of craziness starts to take hold, and all the rules lose force. Those days must be a hell for teachers, unless they are wise enough just to let go and be infected by it too.

So powerful is the recollection that even now, in middle age, though I go to the office as expected and keep up a pretense of devotion to my duties, I can feel the old start-of-summer craziness rise like a tide inside. If ever I do something unexplainable or punishable by law—immolate my typewriter or take to gamboling along public parkways like a *Playgirl* centerfold, garlanded with flowers—probably it will happen in this dangerous season of the year.

The children have noticed me out here and a cry has come down from the window. *"Is there any breakfast in this house?"* one of them demands to know—one of my own, their guest being much too polite.

Last night they watered my vegetable garden. Its dimensions are six feet by 15 feet, a tidy plot in which every leaf is counted. They watered it with the excessive passion of their present mood. An hour ago, in the early light, I found radishes beaten flat and tomatoes drooping and several branches of squash broken over at the joint. I looked on this damage with mild regret but without any anger at all. That's how this time of year commands that everything should be done—immoderately, beyond reason.

A sleek grackle has come waddling with his irridescent mane of feathers to peck among my sodden plantings. May he find something of use or interest there. I'll leave him to it, and go now to answer that command about food.

By mid-morning the girls will be in swimming suits and demanding transport somewhere. By noon, this noon or another, the summer will have passed, and several other summers, too, and there will be boys— the sons of friends, suddenly become louts with predatory eyes and suspicious intent—hanging around the house.

By afternoon, all these children will be gone. Gone off to other places in the world. Waking in other houses of their own, faintly remembering how the tide of summer used to rise. Remembering, perhaps, this very morning.

Time, stand still.

2. *Links in the Food Chain*

We human beings have a boundless determination to idealize the circumstances of our existence. Thus we conceive of hardship to be ennobling and pain to be beatifying, all the more so if they are somebody else's. We honor the willingness to work a lifetime at the same desk in an unrewarding job as a kind of heroism. We have invented the notion of romantic love to explain the commoner impulses of loneliness and procreation that bring us from time to time together.

In this same vein, it pleases us to imagine that a house aswarm with life—grown-ups, children, pets, the more different sorts of life the better, ruling out only mice and cockroaches—must necessarily be a happy and a loving place. But the reality seldom is that simple.

My own household, for example, presently consists of two adults, two children, a dog, six goldfish and one more cat than the law allows.

The cats, shut indoors to stop them from eating the neighbor's birds, sit solemn and attentive with their eyes close to the aquarium glass. The dog lies on a rug not far away, pretending to sleep, waiting for the cats to get careless. The balance of our coexistence is fairly delicate. Seeing them that way—all watching and being watched—I suspect sometimes we are not the loving family our friends think us to be. But that we are instead only a dangerously closed ecosystem. Just links in the protein chain.

The latest addition has been a lizard and, with him, a box of 50 meal worms which on alternate days must be delivered up by threes into his lair. Actually, this one is the second lizard. The first one came home from the country the other day in a bottle. He (she?) was a fence swift, a three-inch creature counting tail and all, with a brown hide like tree bark and the head of a miniature dinosaur. He went into a fish bowl left over from the days before the tank. Earth, moss, rocks and a jar lid of water were provided for his comfort and amusement. A screen was put over the top to hold him in.

Once that first night, when we sprayed the interior of his bowl with a plant fogger, he gave a little shudder that we took for pleasure. That was the nearest we came to any communication. What to feed him was an issue, but not for very long. Because the next morning, shortly after the children left for school, the cats solved the small problem of the obstructing screen and the question of fence swifts' diets became academic.

If you have children, you know how such a crisis—with its prospect of blind tears and brooding hurt—can galvanize a parent to a frenzy of self-interested activity. Inconvenience doesn't matter. Cost is no object. Has a lizard been sighted in some distant state? Quick, fly the damned thing in by hired plane and be done with it! Anything to avoid the scene that otherwise surely will follow.

By day's end, the successor lizard was in place. Not a fence swift but a green chameleon, in a pet-store terrarium made for the purpose, with a light on top and a lid that latches.

Thanks to these exertions and expenditures, life was able to go forward. The furnishings of the death bowl were transferred to the terrarium. Much love already has been invested in its occupant. He has become for a time the center of our lives. He has a name. His habits are meticulously observed and reported in detail. Neighbor children arrive in numbers to admire him and help offer up his ration of worms. Superficially, again, our household seems a loving and untroubled habitat. But even though the immediate crisis has passed, a great sense of danger lingers darkly over me.

For, as I've said, I know how delicate the balance really is. We hang by a thread.

The chameleon eats his meal worms and is unafraid. But I find myself overtaken at odd moments by this cold vision, like a waking dream, of things to come. It is that the cats, having one day finally polished off the goldfish, will solve the terrarium latches, too. And will eat the chameleon.

And the dog, seeing them grow smug and inattentive, will seize that opportunity to eat the cats.

And the children, in grief and fury, will eat the dog.

And the next move will be mine.

A postscript: Returning home from the office immediately after writing the above, I found that, while the latches had not been undone, the terrarium itself had been knocked off the table onto its side in an obvious attempt to break the glass.

So it is beginning.

3. Cat in Crisis

The white cat, Oliver, has slipped off the edge and into his midlife crisis. I have been there, so I know what he is going through.

Some of us announce the event by having nervous breakdowns. Others grow beards, or begin a sly affair. And some, like the stockbroker Paul Gauguin, give up job and family to answer the call of a different career. These remedies are not available to a cat.

He has no way of knowing which of those other households along the street might greet him with a friendly hand, and which with a thrown shoe. He has grown accustomed to sleeping in upholstered chairs beside fires. He knows the exact placement of his food dish, and the sound of the can opener. It is no use to remember the odd mouse caught or bird eaten over the years. Oh, Oliver is good, all right; he is talented in these matters. But a cat on the lam has to be good *every day*.

In a word, then, he is trapped.

There never is any telling exactly what triggers the midlife collapse. In women, it sometimes is said to be caused by the fading of beauty's bloom. In men, by the deline of sexual vigor—although the veterinarian some years ago removed that from the list of Oliver's concerns. In his case, the crisis seems to have been provoked by the arrival in the house of yet another cat, this one a mere kitten. Several previous additions to the menagerie he has endured sullenly, but without violent display. He bears, I think, no special malice toward this small newcomer. But sheer numbers have begun to tell on him. He has finally snapped.

The personality change has been dramatic. He has become a street brawler, a common thug. It's a Jekyll-and-Hyde existence he leads. He does not abuse the kitten. He frowns a lot, but never attacks. And when invited to, he still curls in a lap and purrs as winningly as ever. But let a door stand ajar an instant and he is through it and outdoors immediately, lip curled and spoiling for a fight. Somewhere, evidently, he has located another misanthropic cat.

I don't know how the other fellow looks, but Oliver comes home a wreck. His ears, which used to be so silky-pink, are cut and punctured and crusted now. There is a patch of fur gone from his forehead and an ugly welt across his nose. He looks the way George Plimpton must have after three rounds in the ring with Archie Moore. This has been going on for days—no, weeks—now, and still they haven't settled it. Or maybe there is nothing to settle. I can't say about that other cat, but Oliver, I believe, is fighting just because it feels good. Feels better, at any rate, than simply sitting and staring out windows, brooding on the bad luck that has overtaken him in his middle years.

I tell him that he'll burn himself out.

He comes reeling home at meal time all bloody and moth-eaten. And hunkers down scowling in front of his food dish. And gives the new kitten a long, even look as if to say, *You see what's happened, don't you? You see what's become of me, all on account of you?* Then, after eating and sulking a while, he makes his way to my lap for consolation and advice.

"The thing is," I tell him, "you've got to pace yourself. You're burning the candle at both ends and in the middle, too. Keep on this way and you'll wind up just another punched-out club fighter with funny eyes and headaches before you're 8."

Time is the great healer. One day, eventually, his rage will pass—it always does, with all of us. We accommodate to the changes in our lives and grow placid again. We shave off our beards and return to our spouses and ask for our old jobs back, deciding not to be painters—or, in Oliver's case, a mugger—after all.

It will happen, with patience. But, for now, he lays his tattered ears back flat against his head and leaves my lap with a growl. He already is planning the next battle. He is not quite ready yet to be told about coming to terms with his own limitations and the world as it is. And I understand.

Neither, for a long time, was I.

4. *Coming of Age in Boulder*

Having mastered the elements of rudimentary speech, their first request was for the piercing of their ears. Memory telescopes time, of course—but that is my recollection of it.

I threatened to do the thing myself with hammer and nail. They sobbed in terror but were undissuaded. In one form or other, evidently, it is an impulse as old as the memory of the species. For the *Encyclopaedia Britannica,* under its entry titled "Mutilations and Deformations," catalogues a really dazzling variety of practices—some of them so deliciously depraved as to forbid much discussion here.

"Perforation of the earlobe for insertion of an ornament," the encyclopaedia reports, "is exceedingly widespread." Widespread in *some* circles, perhaps. But not among those dear, kind ladies of probity and virtue—mother, aunts, older cousins, remoter family and friends of family—who filled and supervised my boyhood and shaped my values in ways not later easily unbent.

Pierced ears, while not actually evil, were a little less than decent. Pierced ears were for the saloon, the dance hall and worse. Surely I must have agreed for, while it was not a matter of conscious deliberation,

10

never to my certain knowledge did I date a girl with holey lobes. (Well, maybe one—on the sly.) So I found this demand of my daughters—sweet heaven, of my *babies!*—more troublesome than might a father of different or more cosmopolitan background.

Several years I managed to resist, years of tears and ultimatums. Any number of their little friends were having ears violated. I heard the names recited and was unmoved. But the day their mother had her own ears done I knew I was on a slippery deck.

It happened finally in Boulder, Colo. On a birthday, while traveling. As the alternative to an enormous stuffed dog of serious price and nasty look. Done by a stranger, in a department store, with a two-for-one coupon from the Boulder *Camera*. Their mother the procuress took them and I didn't go to watch—was spared that much. So what I know of the procedure comes second hand.

I had imagined great physical pain. They reported there was little. (I know the ear lobe is supposed to contain few nerves. But the same is said of the scalp and I believed that, too, until once, bending at the wrong time, I caught a thrown horseshoe just above my lateral occipital gyrus.) The surgery, it seems, no longer is performed with a stone and a whetted splinter of bone. There is a machine for the purpose now, something like a staple gun. The operator aligns the cold metal against ear, presses a lever and in a single blinding instant of lost innocence the thing is done—the hole made and the first small silver ornament driven and locked in place.

Less painful than the least bee's sting, they said it was. Hardly a pin prick. They seemed somehow subtly changed, more worldly. We drove away from there fast, leaving stuffed dog and department store and hateful city behind. In Latin societies, too, they pierce the ears of their female children at the earliest age. And consider the birth rate in Latin America.

Still, it is important to be open-minded and progressive, able to change with the times. To that end the other day I called my daughters around me and got down some books, illustrated volumes from past years of travel. Surely, now that they had begun, they didn't intend to call it quits at such trifling perforations. So I opened the books—lay before them a veritable smorgasbord of fashionable self-mutilations—and commanded each to choose one.

Here, for instance, was a fetching style from Kenya, the ear lobes stretched and elongated with weights into leathery loops that were tied together behind the neck for convenience.

"He's kidding," one of them said to the other. But uncertainly, not smiling.

Or consider these giraffe ladies from Burma, necks extended inside wrapped brass coils until vertebrae from the back are drawn well above the shoulders.

"*Groady!*" the other shrieked.

Or this Tubbu charmer from Chad, a ring passed so cunningly through her nose.

"He is kidding." With visible relief.

Or this one with the notched ears and the wooden plates for lips.

"Look, if you want to do that to *your* lips (laughing now) that's okay. But us? No way!"

Wait, wait—they were leaving—*you haven't seen the four-inch golden lily feet of the Chinese!*

But they were gone, all smug and self-contained. A father tries to be liberal-minded and instructive and gets, for his pains, laughter and dismissal. Do they suppose I could not detect, in the manner of their going, just a suggestion of the slinky, swaying coquetry that has always distinguished the ladies with pierced ears? And is it possible that any boy attracted to such a girl could be good enough for a daughter of mine?

5. *The Mannerly Stallions*

My younger daughter, age not quite 10, is beginning to compete. And in the fierce flow of small bodies to and fro over the soccer field she will learn, sooner or later, to draw blood. From all indications, that will be later rather than sooner.

There already are a few—the precocious ones, and large for their years—who have the idea. They are able to accept a kicked ball full in the face and, after pausing briefly to determine that nose and teeth still are in place, to lurch back into the fray, meaning to give at least as good as they have gotten. Around these few the success of the Stallions will have to be built. (It is a peculiar name for a team of fifth- and sixth-grade girls, but you are mistaken to suspect a male chauvinist in the woodpile. They chose it themselves, by democratic vote.)

For the others, of whom my daughter is one, there is a hollow place—a rotten spot of courtesy and deference—where the killer instinct ought to live. They pay honor to a strong kick, not much noticing whether the kicker's shirt is blue, like theirs, or red. They find pleasure in the queer dexterity of anyone able to impart speed and approximate direction to the moving ball. It is an act of beauty which, by and large, they seldom are inclined to interrupt.

To them, the opponents' goal is not something into which one ever actually propels a shot. It is more in the nature of a mythic concept, a splendid abstraction, like romantic love or the ability to speak the language of the French. One does not dream of achieving the goal—else it would no longer be a goal. It is privilege enough simply to draw near.

13

Their own goal, however, the one they are defending, is another matter entirely. The distance between its net posts is at least a day's march. The net itself is like a great mouth gaping with hunger to receive the ball— a sort of logical and inevitable catchment into which everything must be funneled, either by sequential accidents or by the slope of the terrain itself.

When the enemy host comes bearing down, all savage and adept, bleating a barbarian cry, the Stallions—I mean my Stallion and the ones of her nature—all stand transfixed like birds before the snake. I do not know if it is terror that roots their feet in place. It may be pure admirations. In any case, when destiny shunts the ball into the net, as almost always happens, they evince no particular despair. Quite the contrary, they seem almost pleased to have been there to watch it happen.

At the half-time intermission, there are quartered oranges to suck. And at the end of the match, cans of soda pop from the coach's ice chest. This mentor of theirs is a great bear of a man. They have bought him a T-shirt with the legend "Great Coach" printed on the back. But I can tell that like many of the Stallions themselves he is flawed by gentleness. He allows them all to play. He does not rend his garments and assail the officials in the way a truly great coach is duty-bound to do. He is indiscriminate with praise. He speaks of mere effort as if it were a virtue, when what he should be speaking of are the more subtle ways to rip and gouge.

All of which is only to say that he does not put the importance of winning in its correct perspective.

In this latest match my daughter happened to be standing in the way of a cannon shot unleashed by some larger girl. It caromed off her side and left a considerable bruise, rewarding her with the character-building opportunity to play with pain. She smiled. And in my happiness for her, I smiled, too. She is making progress.

14

This is the team's first season, and so naturally it's a building year. With a good weight program, the proper use of steroids and a couple of decent drafts, I see the eventual makings of a contender. The involvement of a few concerned fathers like myself also undoubtedly would be helpful. Meantime, the Stallions are either 0 and 4 or 0 and 5, with the hard part of the schedule still ahead.

6. The Truth-Giver

Primitive cultures transmitted the slender body of known facts about their world from one generation to the next verbally, in the form of myths and folk tales. Now we have libraries and computer memory banks and instructional television and great universities. And in spite of all this, our methods for informing the young really have progressed very little. We still are the oral teachers of those who follow us, and it is truly remarkable that even a few of them manage to grow up with any sensible understanding of the planet on which they live.

The event that brought this to mind was a nature walk the other Saturday in a suburban park with a troop of Junior Girl Scouts—a dozen little girls ages 9 and 10, in credulous pursuit of some badge or other. I went along meaning to be no more than a protective presence on the fringes of the expedition. Instead, I found myself pressed—dragged is the better word for it—into the role of the shaman, the Truth-Giver, the Teller of Ancient Facts. It is a role I have not sought and for which I am unequipped, as became obvious the moment we embarked down a woodland path, my small proteges trailing attentively behind, waiting for the book of Nature's mysteries to be opened to them.

The subject was supposed to be the seasons—in this case the turn from summer to autumn. I sifted frantically through the shallow midden of my memory for information about fall, and found little there. Something happens chemically to the leaves. They change colors and drop. It turns cold. The days grow shorter. There are no more mosquitoes. Colorado ski reports begin appearing in the newspaper. That was the sum of it, pathetic scraps of knowledge you would expect a child to bring home from preschool, at the latest. In desperation then, I elected to discourse upon Nature in a more general way.

A large white rock presented itself.

Do you see this? the Truth-Giver inquired. *You may not know what kind of rock this is.*

"It's a sedimentary rock," came an instant reply.

Yes, as a matter of fact. It's limestone. It is made of the shells of thousand and thousands of tiny sea creatures.

"You mean—" (one of the others) "—that this all used to be covered by the ocean? How long ago was that?"

A very long time ago.

"Could it happen again? How soon will it be?"

Actually, I don't know. That is—I suppose it could. But not right away, I shouldn't think.

Then the first one again, the smug one: "Sedimentary rock is one kind. And igneous is the second, but I forget the third kind. What's the third kind of rock?"

"Let's get out of here!" said the one who was concerned about the ocean.

And we passed on mercifully to a bush.

Perhaps, said the Truth-Giver, *you do not know how plants travel.*

"By their seeds. Some blow in the wind."

"And some stick to your clothes."

Yes, certainly. But how else? A waiting silence. That one stymied them. *Do you see these purple berries? Well, they taste good to animals. So the animals eat them and travel around.*

The Truth-Giver crushed a berry to reveal the seed in its purple ooze.

Then they pass the seeds.

"Pass them?"

Right. In their droppings.

The group, in unison, made a nasty sound with lips and tongues. But the Truth-Giver pressed on, flinging out whatever came to hand from his bag of myths.

These bumpy green balls are called hedge apples. If you put one in your basement it will keep bugs out of the house. And here's an insect's egg case. (Discovering, too late, that it was only some sort of woody deformation on the surface of the leaf.) *Anyway, see this moss? It always grows on the north side of the tree. Which means that this path will undoubtedly lead us back to—*

They emerged from the forest into the parking lot of a subdivision. The lot was in the process of being enlarged. *That's called a bulldozer,* said the Truth-Giver, recovering nimbly. *Seldom encountered in Nature.*

They were, in fact, momentarily lost. *Remember, now. We started out along a stream, didn't we? So if we just make sure to walk downhill—*

"Look, that's the side of the tree the moss is on."

"Yuk! There's a bug on my hedge apple!"

—it is certain to be the right way home. Now isn't it?

And it was. The stream was where it was supposed to be. The Junior Girl Scouts raced ahead toward the cars, their heads no doubt whirling with all of that new, if not terribly useful, knowledge. Driving back to the city, I got to thinking about what kind of world I had presented to them—a world as Franz Kafka might have described it. A nightmare terrain, prowled by animals that left purple droppings from which bushes grew, in which it was advisable to hasten downhill, always headed north, in order to get home before the sea came rushing back again to cover the land.

We have our universities and computers today. But much nonsense still is spoken by those of us who are supposed to know. The girls have qualified for their badges. Now it will take gifted teachers the next 10 years or more to clarify their minds.

7. *A Gift from the Stars*

The starship that wanders through space on a mission to seed the universe with cats has beamed down another alien onto our doorstep. As Edgar Allan Poe is said to have cried, lying wretched in a gutter at the last: *Will it never end?*

We need another cat like the world needs a supervirus born of the mating of Herpes and AIDS. We need more cats like Richard M. Nixon needed more tape recorders. We need cats . . .

Never mind. You get the point.

This one is small and black, but with great galumphing white feet that suggest it could grow up to eat the dogs. A minute after being discovered, the thing was in the house. Another minute or so and it was installed in a daughter's bedroom, already with a food dish, a bed and a litter box of its own. Before a strangled cry could rise in my throat, the discussion had every look of being already closed.

We canvassed the neighborhood by telephone. As soon as we stated our business, voices went chilly on the wire. Nobody knew anything at all about the beast.

Cats? they asked. *What exactly are cats?* So I have posted a notice. People who advertise cats on office bulletin boards invite pity and ridicule. You'd do better offering used shoes and pre-owned underwear. The telephoning and notice-posting are just perfunctory gestures, empty of meaning and without any hope of result. The cat is with us. I have been this way before, and I know how it always ends. So do the other creatures of our household.

The established cats—forgetting that they, too, were foundlings once—crouch at the crack of the bedroom door, sniffing, making awful sounds in the back of their throats. They haven't yet seen the size of those feet. The time will come when they'll wish they'd been more cordial.

I try not to think about what's in the closed room. I do not want to be told of the kitten's endearing antics. I'm pretending this hasn't really happened to me, and that the note on the office board was put there by someone else. By tonight, though, the cat will have a name. Tomorrow, or the day after at the latest, it will have the run of the house, and will be sending up coordinates to the mother ship so that another couple of dozen exactly like itself can be transported down.

Twice before we gave found cats away to friends. And shortly afterward both sets of friends left town without a word. Another time we took out an ad in the newspaper. The only reply was from a lascivious heavy-breather who wanted to drop by sometime when I was sure to be away. There is no use resisting destiny. I grumble, but I have learned—am learning, anyway—to sit back and take what luck brings. What it has brought most often, beginning with two beagles in my twenties and a cat or two a year since, is the promise of never being lonely when I sleep.

It could be worse. The starship could just as easily be sending down crocodiles and copperheads. Cats you can live with. Even a great many cats. Ask me. I know.

19

8. The Monster of Studio 5

As you may have noticed, flesh born of woman does not enter this life with immediate genius for playing the clarinet or French horn. And most attempts to learn can be classified, aesthetically if not in law, as unnatural acts—more unnatural for some than for others. Certain children have flaccid lips and sausage fingers and tin ears. And some are worse than just ungifted.

But never mind that. The fashionable assumption is that anyone in this world can accomplish anything he sets himself to. Its corollary is that any child, regardless of his own will or aptitude, can be made to fit the mold of his parents' hopes. So it is that small boys with spindly shins and eyes wild with terror must strap on pads and run trembling up and down the football fields of the land in pursuit of their fathers' approval. Or that girls still soft with baby fat must be committed to the fearful discipline of East German lady shotputters or Romanian acrobats.

And so it is, too, that each Thursday, in the hour immediately before supper, my daughters are delivered up to the place of their musical advancement. But with the important difference that the idea of lessons was theirs entirely, not ours.

The music school is a warren of small studio rooms in the basement of an instrument company. In the long hallways outside the rooms are metal folding chairs for students waiting to begin their lessons or parents praying for them to end. Once some years ago I was in a slaughter house and I have never forgotten the sound of that. All through the subterranean labyrinth of the music school there reverberates a terrible and many-voiced lament: The strangled grunts of the tuba, the braying of trombone and whinny of cornet, the porcine squeal of cracked reeds and protesting strings. They remind me of the noises of the abattoir, and in a sense they are. For something is being butchered there, too.

Our daughters chose piano which I have discovered is the discreetest of instruments. Mostly their mother takes them to their lesson on Thursday, but I am an occasional substitute. I sit on a chair in the hall and now and then look in through the small window to observe them puzzling out a bar of music or bent in studious consultation with their teacher. The sweet murmur of their playing barely can be heard through the acoustically padded walls of the room.

Not so, however, with the aspirant in the next studio to the left. That one is a student of horn. Which horn I can't say; it is unidentifiable in his hands. The noises he causes to come out of it—the heaving groans and windy gurgles—have nothing at all to do with music. Last week I think he was playing *God Bless America,* and what he did to that song would in some societies be punishable by public strokes.

I always try to sit very small in my chair, very flat against the side of the hallway. I look fixedly at the studio in which my daughters are quietly mastering the piano. And in spite of that, other parents seated along the hall peer wonderingly at the closed door of the horn cubicle, then inspect me with a kind of furtive pity. After each explosion of flatulence from behind the door, I want urgently to leap to my feet and cry out, *Not mine! I don't know who or what's inside there, but it isn't mine! Mine are in the next studio. Mine are the two pianists.*

From time to time during the hour, that studio opens and the teacher, a tall, pale man with a crazy look in his eye, stumbles out and shuts the door quickly on the incredible racket behind him. He stands there in the outer hall, swaying a little on his feet like a fireman who has just fought his way through heavy smoke. He doesn't say anything or look at any of us. He just stares a few minutes blankly at the wall. Then looks at his watch. Then draws up his shoulders and hurls himself back into the room. That man must wonder sometimes at the direction his life has taken, and whether there ever can be any way back.

Just once, in leaving, did I glimpse the monster of studio 5. He turned out to be only a small, roundish boy of 10 or 12 years, trapped in his horn's brass coils, perspiring and hopeless of eye, as much a victim as any of us. Then he sucked in a giant's breath, his cheeks ballooned—and we fled directly up the stairs and out to the car.

As I say, music was our daughters' own idea. They began piano because it pleased them to. They are quite as free to stop. We refuse to make them hostages to our expectations. Their futures must be their own to shape. Not long ago the younger one came home from seeing the motion picture called "The Children of Theater Street," about the famous Russian dancing school in Leningrad.

"I've decided what to be when I grow up," she announced. "I'm going to be a famous ballerina."

We were delighted for her, naturally, and offered our immediate congratulations. But how well did she understand the demands of the dancer's calling? Did she know that, no less than the piano, it would mean a life of unyielding discipline? No more frivolous vacations or idling in the sun by the pool. Only iron devotion to one's art—days, months, years spent flexing at the barre. A punishing prospect, no doubt about it. But that is the price of greatness.

"Well . . . "

She turned the matter again in her mind.

"Maybe then," she said finally, "I'll just be famous on our block."

9. *Life Under Glass*

The children have received a microscope as a gift. No, that's not exactly true. What has happened is that their father has given them a microscope for himself to play with, which he does fairly often and which, as it happens, he is doing now, as he makes these notes.

His knowledge of science—of any science—is embarrassingly slight. But he has become fascinated by the small worlds that can be entered through the instrument's eyepiece. The scope, an inexpensive one, is set now on its lowest power, a magnification of 50 times. A desk lamp laid on its side sends light glancing from a mirror up through the bottom of the slide. Coffee and tobacco, the comforts of travel, are at hand. Today's expedition is into a droplet of water drawn from the murk of a long-abandoned goldfish tank and deposited in the polished depression on the slide. (Experience has shown water from the tap, although more populous than one might wish, to be less interesting than the aquarium's juices.)

Under the lens, that one drop becomes a considerable sea. Things are suspended in it—terrible, spiny clusters that resemble islands of steel wool. But they are inanimate, evidently. Then, at the upper right edge of the optical field, life announces itself. Shift the field a fraction, and a tiny globule of gelatin is seen to thrust out a curious "head" and then to dart away quickly, as if on some remembered errand, in the direction the head is pointed. It goes with purpose, and its speed, on the scale of its environment, is nothing less than fabulous. If memory serves, one of the spiny islands is drifting somewhere to the left, approximately on the creature's course.

23

Shift the field again. Yes, there the thing is. The swimmer seems not to see or sense it there and, as if deliberately, plunges straight ahead into the awful tangle, writhes there a while, and then is still. The whole sea is still as well. For in that droplet not another living thing can be found—only the drifting stalks and fragments of some that might once have lived. Sometimes it is like that. Life does not uniformly teem.

But the next sample, taken from a different sector of the fish tank, is broth of a richer sort. Instead of a single protozoon, there are now whole colonies and cruising schools of them. Animals of a different species, these—lightly speckled, able at will to clench and then elongate themselves in tubular shape, with a fine beard of cilia whirling about what one takes to be a mouth.

The glass depression in which the droplet lies is, to the naked eye and to the touch, ground out and polished to a perfect smoothness. Under the lens, however, it looks quite different. Magnified, its rim becomes a jagged and forbidding coast, distinguished by countless unnamed coves and prominences, broken headlands and shadowed fiords. One of these coastal features might well be named Point Desolation. For there, it seems, the weak and hurt among the swimmers appear most often to be borne up by the tide, to cluster in considerable numbers and finally to die.

An afternoon can easily slip by like that, with the eye held raptly to the scope. One forgets to smoke. Coffee grows cold in the cup, as mine has, and must be replenished. While doing that, the maker of these notes will have to consider whether to tell here—to invite ridicule by telling—something that he has just seen under the glass. The kettle boils now. And, yes, he will tell about it—but in the most factual way. Just the event itself as it occurred, or seemed to, without any discussion of the implications. Without concluding anything.

24

Moving the field of the glass ever so slowly, he had set out from Point Desolation, bearing southeastward down into that quarter of the sea where, on another map, Australia might have been. There he came upon two protozoa of the race described above. Or it may have been one animal in the process of becoming two. First they seemed a mass together, but soon divided either into two individuals or autonomous halves of the one. It makes no difference which.

After proceeding only a short distance, these two blundered into the threadlike tendrils of some filamentous object and commenced instantly to thrash and struggle in an effort to free themselves. Their exertions, which only caused them to become worse entangled, grew progressively more feeble. The outcome seemed obvious. But with a last violent contortion, one of the creatures managed actually to break loose. It darted some little way off and stopped there, its middle parts rising and falling rapidly.

The note-taker duly recorded this behavior, observing—at least to himself—that, were it some other, larger species, the animal might be described as panting with exhaustion and relief. Then he put his eye back to the glass and noticed an unaccountable thing. The free creature, the escapee, had turned again toward the danger zone—had drawn close to the entangled one, actually touching it finally with its forepart but eliciting only a faint movement.

"Look out!" the note-taker cried aloud.

But it was no use. With a slight wrong movement, the creature had come up against a filament again. Another instant and it was entirely enmeshed. The thrashings were repeated, although more briefly. Then a final quiet settled over that zone of the sea.

It was not something one is glad to have seen. And it is not something the note-taker is entirely comfortable to be reporting here. He does not know what it means. He does not *want* to know. That much decided, he will now take a square of paper tissue and dry that specimen slide until it squeaks.

10. *After Frogs*

An anthropologist whose essays I admire has written quite poetically of the emergence of primal, wriggling things out of the ooze at the water's edge to become, eventually, the creature known as man. In some part of us, he suggests, we carry with us always the evidence—and possibly even a sense that is older and more primitive than conscious memory—of our ancestral beginning, an affinity for the marshes. My daughters have not read that man's book. They are only the living proof of its truth.

I was struck the other day by the extent to which the passage of a few years, and a bit of civilizing, can affect one's attitude toward so congenial an element as mud.

Mud is widely known to be one of the sovereign entertainments of childhood. Things can be constructed of it. Pies and cakes can be made with it and these even can be eaten—although usually only once. All else failing, it can be walked in. Then, at a certain age, the charm of all this passes.

On the day I've mentioned, some project had taken us to the farm. And while we adults were occupied with our work, the children, our daughters and a small friend, went exploring at the margin of the pond. The drought of the past summer had caused the water to recede far out from the normal bank, leaving a wide band of exposed bottom, a no-man's-land where reeds stood withered in a slaty crust. Under that deceiving crust, of course, untouched by sun, lay 20 years and several feet of virgin ooze. I expect that you can guess the rest.

From where we worked, we could hear the increasing sounds of joy, the cries of inexpressible delight. These filled us, too, with reassurance and pleasure. Plainly all was well in that direction. Occasionally one of the children would come up to where we were, to issue some vague report. *So-and-so stepped in,* she'd say. Or, *You ought to go see So-and-so.* In our preoccupation, the true meaning of these bulletins was lost on us. "Did she?" we replied abstractedly. "That's nice. Be careful now."

What had happened is that one of them had spied among the reeds on the dry pond floor a distant relative. And, taking another step out, had broken through the crust and into the mire below. Then the others had followed—all of them in pursuit of their frog cousins that leaped and skittered ever farther out across that region of trembling earth. And once shoes have been so horrendously defiled, what more is there to lose? So they gave themselves up entirely to the happiness of their return to the nurturing substance.

In due time our job was finished and we went to collect our young at the pond. Except in size, the slime creatures we saw emerging there can have differed very little from those first protean things that tried their luck on land.

"We were after frogs," they said, as if that explained it all. Which, being an accurate statement of genealogy, in a way it did. Rage and scolding were strangely without effect. Oh, they made the required noises of contrition, but unconvincingly. A look of bliss suffused them. It was as though the mud had called to them with a stronger and older discipline than mine.

Later, with them asleep and their clothes and shoes caking and drying on chairs beside the cabin stove, I turned these speculations in my mind. For just a moment, there in the stillness, it seemed I might connect with something that would bring it all clear.

But then that instant passed. It has been too many years and there are feelings, wisdoms, with which I am out of touch. Intuition is very powerful in the young. Or is it possible that children, being newer from the water, still half-remember what we cannot?

11. Secret Tenderness

The old cat sleeps beside the telephone and has never had a call. Has never had a friend.

She was a lady of the streets for as long as age was on her side. But she waddles now. Her tattered hair skirts drag the autumn ground. Her beauty mark, a notched ear, is wasted on the prowling toms. Other cats have come and gone—undone by years or by the wheels of some indifferent car. The old cat stays, cautious and durable, nested safely amid the clutter of books and papers on the telephone table, from which, with slitted eye, she observes life passing. None in all that procession of other creatures has cared much for her.

The dog waits for her around the corner of the stair. The cats, allies of the dog for purposes of ambush, crouch atop and under and behind the furniture. Returning from some small excursion, the old cat—the friendless one—peers into the darkness of the open doorway and considers the gantlet to be run, measures the distance to her perch. Then makes a dash for it. Out the others come, then, erupting from the shadows in hot pursuit. It's all for sport. They've never caught her and do not mean to catch her. They only want to make her scurry and scramble humiliatingly.

Something about her must invite torment. Does her manner betray the insecurity, the shame, of having once been a winter stray? Whatever the reason, her entries all are the same, all noisy and harried. Even the smallest, clumsiest kitten new to the household soon joins the baying rabble at her heels. She has perfected the art of being inconspicuous. If it were not for our using the telephone, we might forget she lived with us at all. She sleeps a lot, as old cats do. When stroked, or scratched behind an ear, she seems surprised and a bit uneasy. She objects to being held. One could almost suppose that she had achieved so final a state of wariness or disillusionment that affection no longer figured in her plans. And yet . . .

Twice in these years there have been periods when, through some sequence of sad misfortune, the old cat was the only creature remaining to us. The losses left empty places in our house and in our hearts—deficits which the strange, shaggy, reticent survivor moved promptly to rectify. She left her station beside the phone and found the courage to strop herself against a trouser leg. At night she curled at the foot of the bed where one or more of the others had previously slept. It was not so much that her nature had changed. The caution still was there. After having passed so many solitary hours she had no sense of how to be a lap cat, nor do I think she wanted to be.

Her interest in those times seemed less in receiving attention than in giving it. It was as if, responding to our need, she played the pet as best her misshapen temperament would let her. After several weeks, then, the replacement cats would begin to arrive. And immediately—though with no show of pique or resentment—the old girl would return to her accustomed habits, taking up her place beside the phone again, waiting for that call that never comes. And soon the new cats would learn to devil her and lurk beside the door.

These other ones I value for their glossiness or grace or other virtues. The old cat I value for the goodness of her heart. I remember those times when she was not just kept; when she was *needed.* And I am led to think that there must be a great deal of unknown and unsuspected tenderness about, like the consideration in that old cat, waiting only for space and reason to be noticed.

12. *Seed of the Revolution*

In the last week, both daughters have rearranged their rooms and they are elated to discover that, in at least this small respect, they can control their world. Because in so many other things they are powerless.

Except occasionally in restaurants, and sometimes even there, they eat food that is chosen for them. They travel on holidays where we travel. As it happens, they love those places—and love them they must, in any case, or else stay home. They are financially dependent, their allowances a dole whose amount and frequency are decided by someone else. And the dole is subject to threats of being withheld, although that has never happened. The law commands that they be educated. And, once they are delivered up to the school, the teachers dispose of their days and sometimes of their evenings as well. The hour at which they must retire to sleep is fixed. Special circumstances and strenuous appeals may vary it some, but generally speaking it is a rule in whose making they had no part. So they lie down when told to and, whether rested or not, rise up again when commanded.

Life is unfair, a recent President observed. He might have added that childhood is undemocratic.

In the matter of the arrangement of their rooms, however, our daughters have seized control. Not without some grumbling on my part, since I am the beast of burden—the lifter and carrier of beds, the mover of bureaus, the hanger of pictures and mirrors and the plugger of the nail holes where they hung before. One of the girls, disabled by the flu a day or two and with too much time to think, mapped out the new floor plan in her mind. This small assertion of power inspired her sister to do the same.

The plans were unworkable, I said. Logic and function dictated where the articles of furniture must go—logic which had governed the rooms' arrangements in the first place. There was no use tampering with the laws of geometry. But they persisted. So for two nights the beast labored and at the end of that, stepping back to look at the result, had to admit that major improvement had been wrought. The rooms seemed lighter, more spacious. And even more functional. Without exception, their instincts had been borne out and mine shown to be dogmatic and uninspired.

I would not make so much of this, except that it clearly is one of the early steps in a process that will continue and gain greater force in the years immediately to come. For if they are competent now to control the space in which they live, will it not seem to them reasonable that they should exert autonomy in other things? And, eventually, in all things.

The power of parents is the power, first, of sheer size. And then of undoubting trust. And finally of wisdom. Then, on a particular day, in some matter perhaps as small as where a bed will fit, what passed for wisdom is seen suddenly to be capricious and flawed. From that moment, authority begins to come unraveled. And the process, once set in motion, cannot be reversed. Among the subjects of a political tyrant, the result of that discovery is called revolution. On shipboard, it can end in mutiny. For children, with any luck, it ends in whole adulthood.

13. The Predator

Swollen ambition is an alarming thing to see. One morning last week the black and white cat, Eric, appeared at the back door to display his catch, a startled chipmunk, carried quite uninjured by the nape of the neck, the way cats regularly transport their young. He wanted to bring the prize inside. And when that wasn't allowed, he dropped it in dismay. The grateful chipmunk scurried away into its hole, and Eric sulked.

But the adventure has given him an altogether new estimate of himself. The next day, from inside a window, he spotted bigger game. Flat against the sill, shoulders and haunches flexing in an imagined stalk, he watched a pilfering squirrel carry one of my late tomatoes up a tree.

The day after that, it was a fat rabbit. Then the neighbor's Labrador retriever. And then the Monday trash truck. I'm gun-shy, now, about letting him out for his half-hour morning run, afraid he might find his way to the zoo and savage an elephant.

In other ways, he's still a splendid cat. He is good with people. He tolerates being held and has never shown a claw. So, even if he happened to be at large when one appeared, I do not seriously think he would drag down a meter man. But at the beginning of every day, when the house is opened to let in the crispness of that hour, he crouches just inside the door. The golden coins of his eyes stare fixedly at the wilderness beyond the screen. He knows there's more to life than being fed and petted.

Isn't that the restlessness in us all? The merely pretty yearn to be ravishing. The moderately gifted hunger after genius. The man who only has a million wants a billion. The tin-pot politician dreams of being an emperor. The bankrupt republic wants to be a superpower. And now, in overweening vanity, a 14-pound cat imagines himself the master of the block.

"Go for it!" the indoor cats probably are saying, offering this advice from a safe distance in the rear. He's young still, Eric is, and doesn't know the lessons that time teaches. A lot of grief can come from over-reaching. At least that's been my experience. More cats have left this world through reckless arrogance than through humility, I tell him. But he doesn't listen—just waits at the screen on the chance an undefended pit bull or careless Volkswagen might happen by.

14. Breaking the Rules

My daughters recently became the owners of a Monopoly set, and playing the game has laid all our characters bare. We have brought the set west with us for a short vacation in the mountains. At night, when we return from our vigorous excursions, we wolf a hasty supper and draw up chairs around the board. The cabin curtains are closed. A log fire smokes and hisses on the hearth. As the dice roll and we bend to our work, the healthy ruddiness of the day drains from our faces, which become pinched and squinty with greed.

I cannot say that what we find in the game is pleasure, exactly. There are terrible rages. There are sullen disappointments. Occasionally there are tears of hurt and bitter humiliation. Still, the playing of it has come to engross us all. You might almost say to *monopolize* us. The contest never really ends; it is only adjourned from one evening to the next. Betweentimes, the board, the paper money, the plastic houses and hotels and the neat arrangements of our title deeds remain in place on the table. This obliges us to take our meals standing up, or from plates held in our laps, which we gladly do. What is important is the game.

I am, besides being a player, also the Banker—a role which entitles me to handle bills of important denomination. I disburse the payments for passing Go. I am the custodian of unbought properties and the issuer of mortgages. I interpret the rules and preside over the woe of the bankrupt.

It happens that I also have the middle-age disease of early rising. Often, awake alone in the still morning, I examine the last night's board and the relative fragility of my situation. The bank's assets are on the chair next to my own. What if my problems are grave? Is not their solution readily at hand? A property or two retrieved from mortgage . . . a sheaf of currency moved from one stack onto another, *to be repaid later in full, of course.* I do not act on these thoughts, but they pass through my mind. And I cannot help wondering, then, if real-life bankers, astir in some quiet hour ahead of their clerks and colleagues, are not from time to time assailed by these same dangerous notions. They must be. You occasionally read about them in the newspaper.

My wife plays cautiously, is prudent in her acquisitions and favors a robust cash position. During the game's early stages, the stacks of bills mount impressively before her. Her voice is crisp and polite as she collects her tidy rents. Then, later, after Boardwalk or some other high-priced parcel has been developed with hotels, she lands on one of those, her hoard of cash disappears in a stroke, her holdings are disbursed among her creditors and she stumbles demoralized away from the table to write post cards or numbly turn the pages of an old magazine.

One daughter's pattern of play is much like her mother's, although she is noticeably luckier. Bankruptcy is longer coming. The other is a hopeless plunger. She buys real estate with reckless joy. On the very brink of insolvency, she mortgages what she owns to buy more. Her cash reserve shrinks and is exhausted. *"Buy!"* she can be heard to cry, as her empire sags toward apparent ruin. *"Build!"* she commands relentlessly, hocking her last railroad to put one more house on Ventnor Avenue. We try to give her the benefit of our mature counsel, but she persists in this madness. And in the end, she always wins.

Worse, she wins graciously—manages to do so in spite of her handicaps of generosity and tenderness of heart. Two nights ago, before the evening's last throw of the dice, she risked all to save her sister from collapse, buying some worthless tract for an absurd sum. When we left the table she was mired in debt, without liquidity, her borrowing power used up. She had done it, she explained, for no other purpose than to be kind.

To be kind? I followed her to her room. Kindness, I explained carefully, was not the point. The point was to crush and impoverish one's adversaries and to acquire their holdings for one's own. Monopoly was more than just a game. It had lessons to teach about the world, and she'd better learn them well. In commerce, there was little place for kindness. All the same, she said, she would sleep better for having done it.

Never mind, I thought, as I left her and went back to survey the suspended game. Her sin of decency had been a fatal one. Her plight clearly was beyond remedy and the lesson would be learned soon enough.

By rights, the game should have been mine. My luck is better than my wife's and my nature is right for it. I am sensible, yet not opposed to risk if the occasion warrants. I have the killer instinct. But within minutes after beginning the next session of play, the tide turned. My reckless daughter received a windfall. Her properties were redeemed from the bank and more houses were erected on them. Followed by hotels. Each roll of the dice brought new tribute pouring into her accounts. Presently all the real estate was hers, and all the money. She had won again, in spite of kindness. And with some gentle word of sympathy for the fallen, she went off to dream her dreams of untroubled conscience.

Something has gone wrong—grotesquely wrong. There is no mention in the rules of decency and compassion. That is not how Monopoly is supposed to be played. That is not how the game is played in life. As far as I can tell, the lessons she is learning about the world are all the wrong ones.

15. *The Farther Mountain*

Already the sharpness of late autumn has come to the high country. Dawn arrives in stillness under a sky of purest blue. But by mid-morning the wind has freshened, whining at the cracks of the cabin door. A haze of gray has moved across the sun, and weather can be seen gathering around the peaks.

One day last week a storm overtook us on a trail above 12,000 feet. And as we huddled together in the shelter of a rock ledge, the rain changed to something white and more substantial—something undecided between being sleet or snow. The winter is that close. So brief is the mountain summer that, in the highest alpine meadows, soon to be silent white, spring wildflowers still are blooming. But, then, the fact has always been that all seasons pass with a rush.

As I write this, I can see through the window a small group of people outside another cabin some distance away across the hillside. Binoculars show them to be a golden-haired child of 2 or 3 years, the child's parents and an older couple, surely the grandparents. In spite of the breeze and coolness, they have moved chairs and a bench outside to take what there is of the hazy sun. The grandfather is clowning for the child. With a walking stick he hobbles lamely in a circle, mocking age, mocking himself. Someone brings a camera and they all arrange themselves. The child will remember, and some year, no longer a child, may even come back to this place with children or grandchildren of his own. Very soon, that will be.

Their camera is one of those that delivers instant photographs. They all bend close and pass the pictures from hand to hand, reassured—if only for that moment—to have stopped the season's rush.

In past years we hiked and climbed alone, my wife and I. Our daughters remained below in a day camp, complaining of the company and grumbling about the meanness of the lunches we packed for them. Finally, they rebelled. Refused flatly to be left. And at ages then only 7 and 8 achieved their first modest mountaintop—caught something of the passion of it. And now, if we are honest, we must admit that their legs, though still small, can carry them anywhere ours will go. They have crouched, cold and wet, with us and gnawed cheese and apples beside a black lake in the steep bowl where a glacier was born. They understand that getting to such places requires a certain price of pain. And, after having paid it, they heal faster.

Last evening we came stumbling off a 10-mile mountain trail, almost at dark, and ate a silent supper and fell in bed. Today I am recuperating, but they already have flung themselves into some activity or other. I sense the time coming, sooner than any of us would have thought, when they will lead and we will follow if we can.

Shifting just a bit from where I sit, I can see— rearing above and behind a rank of nearer ridges—the summit of a mountain I came this year fully intending to reach the top of. That great rock is blue with distance and frosted with a dusting of new snow. Being a realist, I very much suspect now that I will never climb it. The uncertainty of the weather will be my excuse this year. Next year I will find another. With all these explanations, the rushing seasons will fly.

It may be that some day, leaving me below with a sack lunch and proper supervision, one of my daughters will climb that mountain. Or both of them will. I consider it not sadly at all, but with great satisfaction. That, after all, should be the entitlement of every generation: The chance to win its own summits and stand places its predecessors could not go.

16. Changing Schools

Enough time has passed that I no longer remember in any detail the childhood experience of changing schools. I vaguely recall—or think I do—a bleak interval of nausea on morning waking. But was it measurable in months or weeks, or only days?

I expect I could recognize even now, even through the mask of years, the face of the teacher who struck my knuckles repeatedly and savagely with a ruler for writing with the left hand. Except for those fragments, though, that whole year has been represented by an utter blankness where memory ought to be. Now a daughter of mine has been overtaken by just such a crisis of change. And through her I have been put in touch again with certain of those old feelings I had managed to lock from mind.

Summer was worst. Pain imagined is always more terrifying than pain itself. Her world of friendships, of small alliances, of places and objects known, was doomed to be dismantled and rearranged. Her dearest classmate also was changing schools—but to a different one. During the daytime these awful facts could be forgotten in the giddy whirl of summer's play and busyness. But at evening, and especially at bedtime, they came crowding back again. She speculated on the future the way a condemned prisoner speculates about what might lie on the far side of the executioner's blade.

There hung over her, more than anything, the expectation of loneliness—a dread of such power as to make smiles abruptly vanish and cries of momentary pleasure trail away into moans of remembered grief. Not once in summer, when she and her friend managed to be together, did I hear her on parting speak the word *Goodbye*. Its meaning had changed. It had become freighted with too much finality.

Now summer has passed and the date with the future has been met. Wearing new sneakers, she has gone into the alien world, not daring even to hope she might find her way. The geography of the new school is strange. Its rules are unfamiliar. Her classmates are, as yet, only acquaintances. And the novelty of all this coincides with—worsens—the alarming differences she has begun to sense and see in herself at a changeling age of girlhood.

Eventually, one supposes, new friends will come forward out of those ranks of unknown faces. Rare is the time, and mean the place, where that does not sooner or later happen. Her own virtues will be discovered, as will her demerits. She will be known for what she is and what she is not, which is essential to the comfort of belonging. Best of all, perhaps, she will come to understand that entry into this new world does not require her to leave the old one entirely behind; that change is not necessarily loss; that where she has come from is no less real a place than where she is or happens to be bound for.

The realization of that is important to a traveler of any age, whether the passage is to a distant land or only into some uncharted region of experience. Without it there can be no safety, no coherence to a life. I think she may already be sensing that. For just the other evening, when she and her friend, that old and abiding friend, had spent some hours together, they were able for the first time in many weeks to speak aloud the hateful word.

"Goodbye," they said to one another, quietly and cautiously at first. And found, to their mutual surprise, that it had been emptied of danger. In the course of a friendship, goodbyes are only commas after all, not closings of the book. In the blue dusk, then, they could be heard to cry the word again and again, from yard to receding car. Joyfully—as if it were an affirmation. As if, by speaking it fearlessly, they denied its power to intervene between them.

Change is still threatening. Her world still is in disorder, her smiles less frequent than they used to be and will be again. But on that evening she made a start.

17. Customs of the Tribe

The metal-faced ones come out singly and in pairs and groups from the school door to the car, and when they smile their spun-steel smiles the glare is blinding. My older daughter has joined the Metal-Faced Ones. Her sister, who is younger by a year, will follow in the spring.

This pleases them hugely. The wiring of their mouths is not merely a sign of social arrival. Current wisdom holds it to be indispensable to a normal girlhood, like fluids and nourishment and pierced ear lobes and the mastery of French.

Beyond doubt, society's standards of beauty have grown more exacting. When I was young, and all of us were less lovely, braces were for the remedy of gross deformities. Children whose teeth protruded so radically as to frighten dogs or be a hazard on a crowded bus were carted off to the orthodontist. Anyone able, with whatever difficulty, to whistle or eat an apple was spared.

How to account for the intensity of the present interest in dental correction? Is the national jaw deteriorating? Have dentistry's advances made possible the discovery of problems earlier overlooked? Could it be that, as a group, orthodontists have cultivated more lavish tastes in foreign travel? Or that, there simply being more of them in practice now than formerly, it has become necessary—as a practical matter of economics—to diagnose more alarming overbites?

Never mind the reason; the pressures have grown very strong. Whereas, when looking upon my daughters' faces, I have seen only surpassing charm, keener eyes evidently have observed shocking disfigurement. And as the number of Metal-Faced Ones has grown, teeth without wires have become the stigmata of cruel disadvantage. So the appointment was duly made and the apparatus installed.

They hurt. braces do—at least for a while. But like the pain that immediately precedes sainthood, it is exquisite to endure. The newly beatified are immediately identifiable, mouths swollen and misshapen, cracked lips working and writhing over the wires. The Metal-Faced Ones receive supplies of wax, which may be packed over the teeth to lessen the abrasion. Globules of the wax fall to the floor, stick to the shoes, are trodden into carpets. When the lips are drawn back to expose that waxy oval in simulation of a smile, the effect is ghastly. There is only one other place I know where you see smiles like those. It is in the interior of the Cameroons, among a people who subsist their whole lives eating a gray paste called *fufu* and who have not yet received word of the invention of the toothbrush.

My daughter came home from her first appointment and I knew she was my daughter. I recognized the clothes. Now, in a surprisingly short time, I have forgotten how she used to look; have come to feel a certain affection for her new face; have learned to kiss with caution, lest one of us gets cut; have grown used to the chinking and chiming of metal when she speaks. One day, months from now or years, all that iron will fall away and she will be again transformed. She may smile a stranger's smile, but it will be a smile of such perfection as to give young boys a sudden weakness in the knees.

Meantime, the orthodontist will travel well and widely. And my interest also will be served. For her braces advertise me—along with other fathers of the Metal-Faced Ones—as someone to be reckoned with, to be taken seriously.

Men of other cultures festoon their women with strands of cowrie shells or gold bangles, or put rubies in their noses. The whole sum of their worldly means may be exhibited so. Then, when they are seen to pass, others will say: *There is a man of substance.* That is the aboriginal purpose of such displays, and people are the same the world over. It just happens to have become custom among men of my tribe to put their fortunes in their daughters' mouths.

18.   On the Road to Sudbury

The mathematics teacher does not look like a fiend. In fact, she is a strikingly handsome young woman, clear of eye, wholesome of manner—an unlikely candidate for the devil's work.

Each week in this teacher's class there is written on the blackboard or distributed on a ditto sheet a problem the students may undertake to solve for extra credit. These exercises are not, strictly speaking, mathematical. Rather, their purpose is to expand the logical powers of young minds. They go like this:

The first customer buys half the rabbits in a pet store. The second customer buys 13 rabbits. The third customer would like to buy nine rabbits, but he wants all-white rabbits, and two-thirds of the remaining ones are spotted. Then the first customer brings back one-fourth of the rabbits he initially bought. Three of those are spotted and seven are all-white.

And so forth. I work here from memory of what I saw on the chalkboard the night of open house, and probably my memory is inexact. But you get the idea. Applying logic to the information that is supplied, you are supposed to be able to know how many ducklings were in the cage next to the rabbits. A full week is allowed to find the answer. The involvement of parents in these exertions is not only permitted; it is encouraged. One isn't required to participate, you understand. That depends entirely on whether you love your children and want them to succeed scholastically and in their later lives.

The extra-credit problem for this week is a hand-drawn map of 23 towns connected by a network of roads. One town is designated as the starting point of the journey, another as the destination. The object is to proceed from start to finish, visiting each town only once and never passing twice along any stretch of road. The map seems very innocent and straightforward. But, like the gentle manner of the teacher, it is deceiving. That piece of paper is an instrument of Satan. The trip it proposes cannot be made.

We tried all one evening, my daughter and I, until I whined and wept with frustration and she turned away from me in disgust. I had scribbled on the map until it was hardly legible, and had to do a tracing of it on another paper against the light. In the morning I rose early and bent over the map until it was time to go to work. There I brought the resources of industry into play, turning out 50 copies of the tracing on the office Xerox machine. One by one I spoiled those.

I have come to hate the towns on that map, all of which have cute New England-ish names like Barre and Putney—all self-consciously quaint. And I have sworn never to go to New England on the chance that I might come upon a real village bearing one of those names and lose my self-control, maybe run amok.

The right-hand side of the map can be traveled easily enough. The towns there are farther apart, and there are clues. The left-hand side, however, is a web of roads and a cluster of hateful habitations. With unremitting effort and $25 worth of photocopying, it is possible to visit all of those—except one. You can go to Sudbury, missing Manchester. Or Manchester can be reached by leaving Sudbury out. To arrive at both of them, one short segment of roadway must be traveled twice. *Who wants to go to Sudbury in the first place?* I wonder. Probably it is some wretched hamlet whose cheerless inhabitants still practice the burning of witches. God forbid that I should ever have to go there. If I do, it will be for the single purpose of delivering the mathematics teacher into their hands.

The week will be up at midnight. After that it will be useless to go either to Manchester or Sudbury. But it is Friday for a few more hours yet, and we still have a dozen or so copies of the map. So I bend again to the damnable paper. My heartbeat is irregular with anxiety and fatigue. The roads shift and blur before me. But in my devotion to mathematics and my child, I stumble on, passing through Manchester for perhaps the five hundredth time, Sudbury, like true wisdom, forever unreachable ahead.

19. *The Lion in Autumn*

The cats sit in the windows and observe the changing days. The light shortens and cools. The year is turning. Meantime, the children have noticed another change—not of seasons, but of relations among the cats themselves. Like you and me and all of us, the cats are creatures in time. And time moves on.

In their closed society the white cat has ruled, believing himself born to it. He is much the largest, his heavy footfalls audible on the carpeted stair. Except for the woolly, notched-eared one who only sleeps, he also is the oldest. The others have deferred to him, as well they might. He is—or has been—the lion of the house.

But that is changing now. He has an ailment. Not a threatening one; just humiliating. At intervals, some defect in his internal chemistry causes him to lose the hair on his underside. His skin in those times is smooth and pink. An injection by the veterinarian starts the hair growing again and, for a time, his majesty is restored. But in the hiatus. while waiting for the pinkness to be covered, he is sulky and much ashamed.

This evidence of weakness, even if it is only cosmetic, has not escaped the attention of the other cats. And one of them, a few years younger and drunk with the possibility of power, has begun to try to change the hierarchical order of things. He does not, the children note, much look the part of a king. He is a spotted cat, with a receding brow and a black valentine on the end of his nose. Until the age of 5 he was afraid to go outdoors. He eats dog food and hides on the overhead basement pipes.

A cat like that is hard to take seriously. But, espying what he understands to be a frailty in the ruler, he has begun taking *himself* seriously, and that has made all the difference. Just now, for example, the spotted one gave reckless chase across the living room. The white lion withdrew—but only in tactical retreat. Only to the shelter of a small table where, protected from the flanks, he turned to stand his ground, considering the upstart with a level yellow stare. Age has its compensations, among which is craft. It is one thing to covet a crown, and quite another thing to take it. *When you strike at a king,* Emerson was heard once to advise, or words to that effect, *you'd better finish the job.* History is full of the obituaries of pretenders who ignored that counsel.

The white one emerged, then, and turning his back in huge disdain stalked off deliberately and bounded to the window ledge again and frowned out, only slightly pink-stomached, at silver leaves atremble on the wind of a season drawing down. The spotted rival loitered aimlessly a while, then went down to the basement and his catwalk of plumbing pipes, there to brood in darkness and remember what he could of Emerson. That old cat has a fight or two left in him still. How many, who can say? The unsureness of the others on that point will serve him well.

Some of the same verities govern all of us, cats and people alike. And one of those is that timing is everything. *My time will soon come,* the spotted one is thinking in the dark.

Yes, and so is winter coming, thinks the king, watching leaves curl and fall in the shortening light. *But not yet, my friend. Not quite yet!*

20. The Random Gatherer

There is a defect in me. To wit, the utter lack of any inclination to sort and classify. That is far from the only defect, but it is one I can speak about.

At some point in my education the specific disciplines of the collector were omitted. And clearly they can be useful. Displays of rare butterflies behind glass make interesting wall pieces, although they are distinctly less lovely than the commonest butterfly passing alive across a meadow. I have seen collections of antique barbed wire which, while hideous, were of great value.

But I do not collect. I only gather. Somewhere in a box in a drawer there are some coins that came home with me more than 25 years ago from a long journey through Africa. I never bothered afterward to separate and identify them—just dumped them in the box together, the loose change of a splendid adventure. I have no idea, now, from which exact places the individual coins came. But when sometimes I have jingled them in my hand, they have called up collectively a rich memory of desert moonsets and teeming black cities and the smoke of cooking fires at dawn along forest pathways. And, for me, that has been enough.

The defect remains, however, and is real. And it is obvious that care is being taken to ensure today's children will not grow up similarly flawed. My daughter and her elementary classmates have science projects shortly due. The assignment is to make a collection of 25 examples. Examples of *what* is not important. Twenty-five of anything will do nicely.

These forays at the cutting edge of scientific inquiry can be more difficult than they sound. Several years back, at a different school, we were faced with a similar enterprise. And we decided—for the fun of it, and also as an editorial statement—to make a collection of animal droppings. Immediately, it seemed, all the wild creatures suspended their bodily functions. The project this time is simpler and more discreet. We are collecting and identifying seeds. Again, however, a problem has arisen.

When the display is assembled, the plant from which the seed is taken will need to be described both by its common name and by its Latin one. From a source book we have written out a list of the kinds of seed-bearing vegetation apt to be found in our yard, and the list far exceeds the required 25. The rear yard is a jungle, every bit as suggestive of Africa as those coins in the drawer. Some of the weeds that grow there are considered by statute to be noxious, and harboring them exposes the property owner to penalties of law. Never mind, risks have to be taken in the name of science.

This year, for whatever reason, the weeds failed to flower and fruit. Now in the fall, inexplicably, the plants are barren. The bindweed produced no pods, the beggar-ticks no ticks, the thistles no thistledown. The heads of the Johnson grass are entirely empty of seed. So we are stymied. The date for the project's completion is bearing down. We may have to take another run at animal droppings, after all. But we are not alone. All through the neighborhood, in as many houses as there are children in that class, families just like ours are caught up in frenzy and despair.

And yet, as every parent knows, it is all worth the trouble. For someday, long after she has put schooling aside and gone out into the world, my daughter will find herself in some socially or professionally trying situation. Quite effortlessly, then, across the years, the Latin name for Jimsonweed or possum dung will spring to her lips and she will dazzle and amaze all those around her.

The investment in young minds is never wasted.

21. *Rufus*

He is just a pup, hardly more than three months old, but already full of fire and promise. Too full of fire to suit the old dog, who growls at him but does not bite, and whose empty threats have become unconvincing. He nips at her legs and runs along behind, her tail in his jaws. He poaches at her food dish and brazenly filches her bones.

She looks at us sad-eyed, the old dog does, as if to say, *What's this you've done to me in the ripeness of my years? What does it all mean?*

She cannot remember herself at that age—chewer of shoes, sly defiler of carpets, relentless bedeviler of the cats. Or if she remembers, she does not admit. The years have filled her up: The children's growing, our history in the house, country weekends and delicious wallowings in mud or worse. Short of wind, overtaken by portliness, she had imagined her life ahead as a succession of tranquil days, enlivened only by her once-daily obligation to announce the postman's passage. Now, horrifically, she finds herself with a family to raise.

It has been a long time—years, actually—since I began with a new pup. Other dogs have come to me, half-grown strays or castoffs, and have stayed to be indispensable friends. Two of those, two beagle brothers, stayed 14 years and saw me into marriage and fatherhood. This pup, Rufus, is of a pointing spaniel breed. All the tendencies of both the lines seem to have passed to him intact.

He already is pointing a quail wing staunchly, stylishly, for as much as a minute before, in a victory of temptation over will, he gathers himself to pounce and the wing has to be snatched away. When it's gone, he courses over the grass with a fury, hoping to come upon that beguiling scent again. That is the pointer in his ancestry. But he also displayed an early interest in his water pan—not for drinking from, but for climbing into. The first time he saw a pond, a largish pond, he swam across it. Now he has a plastic backyard kiddie wading pool, in which he thrashes happily and from which he retrieves thrown balls with unrestrained delight. That's the spaniel in him.

Where the crocodile got in I can't say. Much of the time he seems all pink mouth and needle teeth. His world is divided into two categories of objects, those made of tempered steel, and thus not edible. And all the rest.

Sometimes, seeing him at play, it is hard to imagine him ever being of any serious use. But then that evening hour comes, when the old dog is upstairs asleep and Rufus and I go out for a few purposeful minutes together in the yard. I give him the quail wing to hold in his mouth before we start, to remind him of the business at hand. In that moment, strangely, the puppy manner leaves him altogether. He holds the feathered thing gently in his mouth. An expression of great solemnity passes over his face. I think he is in touch, then, with the sense of what he is and will be. I think he knows the future he contains—of cold mornings and crisp leaves and beddings in the back of cars and the glitter of birds' eyes in the instant before they burst from the grass.

There are not many things able to tempt a man, in middle age, to wish the seasons forward, to wish time away. But now, with Rufus, I yearn ahead.

22. *A Higher Destiny*

In recent days we have begun taking in worms. Yes, it has come to that. First stray dogs and cats, then lizards and fish, then turtles, land crabs and neighborhood children. Now worms.

The initial specimens were bright green and horny at one end. The man in the tobacco barn where we picked them up called them tobacco worms. If we'd found them on tomato plants, he said, the same creatures would properly have been called tomato worms. Like the dung beetle, we are what we eat.

But call them, for convenience's sake, tobacco worms. We found a container for them and, disregarding the surgeon general's warning, provided them with their ration of the weed. They gave no sign of noticing their new surroundings. The food was what they were used to. They seemed entirely content to get on with the business of becoming. What they will become, if the tobacco farmer knows his worms, is a moth of the family *Sphingidae*—hawkmoths, or sphinx moths, as they sometimes are called.

In this stage of their lives they gnaw bitter leaves and are loathsome to the touch, their beauty, again according to the tobacco farmer, perceived only by channel catfish. *("You just about have to hide behind a tree to bait your hook!")* But the best is ahead. In another season they will be nectar drinkers. Ungainliness forgotten, they will come riding on agile wings, swift as birds, silent as shadows. And they will own the dawns and summer dusks of the garden, taking nourishment from the throats of only the sweetest flowers.

Not many days later, on a country road, I came across a different worm. A bigger variety, the size of your largest finger, pale chocolate in color, with rows of bright crescent markings down the sides. This new one's future is a mystery. He was crossing the pavement, so his leaf of preference is unknown. He lives in a bottle beside the others. And leaves of several kinds have been supplied, in the hope that he may find one or another of them palatable and so be enabled to continue his slow march toward the destiny that lies on the far side of a long sleep. Even as a worm, that one is quite beautiful. What he might become in his final transfiguration can only be imagined. But surely it will be something very splendid.

We watch, now, for other worms. When driving, we find it hard to raise our eyes from the rushing surface of the road. The nights are chilly. Before the freeze, any creeping thing that means to live to achieve a finer state of being had better be about survival's business. The last leaves must be quickly eaten, the twig found, the cocoon spun. At every hand, in these far, clear days and brittle evenings, one can sense— if one does not actually hear—the cumulative stir of all these hasty becomings.

And if one is a realist, it is necessary to wonder: *What has any of this to do with me?* For, search as I might, I can detect in myself no amazing possibilities waiting on the other side of winter. To wish for wings, if one hasn't them already, is both pointless and painful. If I creep now, and am what I eat, I will not learn to fly.

That is what the worm must think, too, if it thinks at all. The difference is that the worm is wrong.

23. *The Strange Celebration*

Time answers many of the hardest questions, which is as good an inducement as any for living to the middle years and beyond. For a child, some of the most perplexing of those questions have to do with funerals. And in particular, the mystery of how it is that, after hearing the solemn words spoken, people sometimes draw together in a spirit that, if not quite happiness, is a convincing mimicry.

The other day there was a funeral out of town—for someone important to my daughters' memories of all their childhood. I am forbidden to be more specific than that. They have come of an age to know how many private things find a way into what I write and their grief in this case, they have sternly notified me, is too great for public sharing. So I can only say that the service was for a lady in her 80s, a lover of the northern waters, a good fisherperson, a fine story teller, a fierce believer in many causes, a speaker of humor and truth. Something of girlhood endured in her unchanged, so that small people instinctively drew near. And among the most desolate mourners at her service were more children than will even know the names of most of us when we've attained that age.

We drove there on a brilliant morning, the autumn colors aflame, the sky pale and deep, the earth lightly brushed by the season's first snow. We sat, each one wrapped in various thoughts, while the minister spoke. And after that we went to the house. There was much food and a little of the light, innocent wine that she had enjoyed. Out of our interior silences conversation quickly rose. Of other times remembered. Of incidents long ago grown into legends of the clan, and repeated now. Of the various happenings in our lives since last

53

that group was all together—then, also, for a funeral. Of trips and work and politics and crazy plans.

The silences in the house grew fewer. Laughter began to be heard. And it was this—the laughter—that afterward troubled my daughters so. What did that mean? What had become of grief? How could the central fact of the day so soon be set aside? We explained, but not very successfully, that life does proceed. A ceremony like that day's, for such a person, celebrates not only all that has been but also all that, because of it, will yet be. The lady herself had been wise and realistic. She, as well as any, had been able to see beyond sorrow.

A day or two later we were with other friends when talk happened to turn to the subject of rituals, the importance of them. All the occasions of faith and custom and formal celebration that bring us together from time to time in a common frame, of which a funeral is one. These do more than mark the passage of years. They provide a kind of matrix in which to conduct our lives. They testify to that continuum of which each human being is a part, or needs to be. The past is represented there—and it speaks of all one came from. In the presence of children, even children not one's own, the future is guaranteed. One is part of something larger and longer than any day of ecstasy or grieving. One belongs in the moment, yes. But one belongs also to moments unremembered and others waiting to unfold.

Now that is an odd notion to ask a child to understand. My daughters are far from satisfied, yet, to know how it is that anyone can utter laughter on such a day. We have been able to tell them only—and uselessly for now—that in some other year they will find it easier, and a more durable tribute than any flower.

24. *Time for Caring*

There is, among the creatures we patronizingly call "dumb," a surprising amount of understanding. Call it only intuition, if you like. But, by whatever name, the display of it sometimes is amazing.

The white cat, Oliver, met misfortune the other day and came home groggy and disabled. It was, luckily, a problem whose effects would pass. But for that day and several afterward, he was a deplorable case, unable to stand and walk or even, at first, to raise his head. We installed him in the bedroom on a pallet of towels with a cover over him for warmth. From his nest, he peered out helplessly, eyes lusterless and confused.

Evening came, the hour when the bird dog is brought in from his fenced backyard run to enjoy the touch of hands and take his greater ease in upholstered chairs. He's a rowdy, that pup. Sly thief of food from the old dog's bowl—the same food as his own, but tastier for being stolen. And a joyous bedeviler of cats.

Now, Oliver, the white cat, in the fullness of his powers, is nothing to be trifled with. He's a heavyweight in the Marciano mold. The sound that issues from his chest when he's annoyed can turn a challenger's blood to ice. But that's when he's himself. The pitiful thing in the towel bundle was perfectly defenseless. So how would the others respond? Would they take it as a time for settling accounts? And how about the bird dog, especially? He bore no grudges that we knew of. But his one gait is an incorrigible romp, badly suited to a sickroom. We took the chance, though, and let him in.

One bound inside the bedroom door and he stopped. Just stopped stock-still, then sat—nose thrust slightly forward to identify the patient, his face (for animals'

55

features can be wonderfully expressive) mystified and grave. Sitting, the pup raised one forepaw as if to playfully box. There was no motion from the bundle. The glazed eyes remained slitted nearly shut. The paw was lowered and the dog sat a moment longer, considering.

You have read, perhaps, how elephants will stay with a stricken member of the band and, even after death, will use their trunks to try to urge the fallen individual to regain its feet and continue on the march. Well, that's just what the dog did next. He drew close on soft pads, reached out his nose and, with a gentleness quite uncommon for him, administered several little nudges that said, plain as anything: *Get up. It's wrong to see you lying there so still. I'll bet you can get up if you'll only try.*

At the moment, though, the white cat was beyond any such effort. He just drifted in his daze, and gave no sign. Whereupon the dog lay down exactly beside him, parallel and very near, but with face turned a bit sideways so that he could notice any stirring. At that moment, for whatever reason, he preferred that place on the floor to the softness of his usual chair. My wife came up from downstairs, then, and reported the strange behavior of the other cats. Like most of their kind, they're individuals and not much on collaboration. They keep a civil distance, although that's not how she had just found then.

"They're all sitting on the hall carpet," she said. "Close together, in a kind of circle, as if they'd been talking it over."

It can get crowded, sharing a house with so many others of such different wants and shapes. Crowded, and sometimes inconvenient. But two legs or four, clever or dumb, we're there for one another when caring's of any use.

25. *October Night*

Leaves on a midnight street, running ahead of the wind, agile and brown as the massed runners in some Levantine demonstration, shouting a dry slogan, passing under the street lamp and on away deeper into October.

Squirrel's footfalls on the shingle roof, hurrying to or from a barren branch where the nut no longer hangs. Wildfowl riding down the long slant of the season, crying to one another and to sleepers a far song that is sometimes heard and sometimes only dreamed.

Cat squinting from a chair. Other and less lucky cat mewing cold at some closed door.

Bird asleep on a wire.

Owl's hooded eye fixed on something that moves in the moonstruck grass.

Train's whistle hooting faint from beyond cities and across many stubbled fields.

Cattle in a fold of pasture, bedded close together.

Lonely people, bedded far apart.

Gardens withered. Seeds saved.

Despairs all suddenly forgotten. Joys remembered and numbered now in the silent dark. Other things remembered, too. The oddest confusion of them.

Leaf fires smelled a long time ago. And the voice of the stadium crowd on a frosty night. And the feeling of being young—the *exact feeling* of it. And the feeling of first remembering that feeling as something not quite any longer true. The terrible attraction of maps, maps being feasts in prospect. And the way in which, unnoticed as it happened, the passion for going became a passion for going home. But home to what, exactly? And then that question answered.

And the answers to it sleeping now under the very roof whose shingles the squirrel crosses on his pointless errand. In the house where the cat squints from his chair. Beside a bureau in whose drawer the seeds are saved. In a room whose window looks down on the crowds of leaves shouting dryly as they run with the wind on past the street lamp and out of view.

October is a memory and a summation. As with anything concluding, it pays to notice the details.

II.

26. *Luck of Strays*

A bitter wind whispers at the door crack. Sleet rattles like birdshot against the pane. The afternoon gives way to frozen nightfall of a winter arrived too soon, and all creatures alive are divided again into those who have a home to go to and those who haven't.

Yesterday I saw a man in a torn green raincoat—a gaunt man with gray hair flying and strips of blanket bound for warmth around his legs—go in the door of a public library. He had a look of purpose, like someone who couldn't wait to read. But what drew him to that place, you could be fairly sure, wasn't books. It was the hope of a saving hour or two of warmth before his long ordeal in some lonely corner of the night. And it struck me that although he was not so different, except in luck and circumstance, from a hundred other men I know, he bore no record of his past, and the future could no more be seen in him than in the forlorn birds that fly down stiffly from somewhere to peck and fluff at the feeder.

The supply of cats and dogs we keep around us ranges, at any given time, somewhere between sufficiency and scandal. And most of those have been accidental friends. Anything that presents itself at our door can count on coming in. Its past recedes. Its future assumes the immediate shape of food bowls and beds or radiator tops to sleep upon. Provided, of course, that what appears at the door walks on four legs. Old men in green raincoats with rag-wrapped shins we don't take in.

We think, especially in such weather, of all the ones who *haven't* come to us. You spy them sometimes, ghosting sharp-ribbed among the crates and cartons of some alley or eyes reflecting at the edge of the car's headlights from the tangled grasses of a winter ditch. They are all the unnamed, unnumbered kin of the ones we keep and feed. Take them inside and in a day, a week, they would be indistinguishable from any of the others, shouldering for a place on the bed's corner, demanding their rations on time. Just as the homeless staring out of news photographs from some place of pain and ruin are the direct kin of children who sleep between sheets and get braces on their teeth . . .

Just as the gray man in the green raincoat, with blanket-bandaged legs, is no different in any important way from the gray man in necktie and warm topcoat who sees—or doesn't see—him shamble past.

It's the habit of the lucky to confuse luck with virtue. Whether dogs or cats or men, the ones who have gotten in—the well-fed and warm—listen at the door crack, growling at the footfalls of those others still outside, those less-worthy who are passing in the storm. But virtue's rarely the difference. More often it's blind circumstance that leads some wanderers to safety or, on a sudden cutting winter blast, blows the others by.

27. *The Arrogance of Tidy Folk*

I am sick and tired of hearing people say they already have finished their Christmas shopping, when I can't even begin shopping for Christmas until I've found something for my wife's birthday. Her birthday was three days before Thanksgiving. People who have Christmas neatly wrapped up and tucked away under the tree with 12 days still to go are people who were potty trained too early. They are Type-A compulsives, who keep spotless houses and tidy lawns and have clear plastic slipcovers on their upholstered living room furniture.

Speaking of trees, we have looked at the calendar and programed the putting up of ours between 6 and 8 p.m. on Monday, December 30. We like to go to the country in the station wagon to cut the tree at the farm. But the wagon is dead at the curb, and the 30th looks to be the first free day after it is scheduled to be repaired. When the tree is up and decorated, we will make a photograph of our daughters smiling in front of it. We will pose them in such a way as to hide the fact that there are not yet any packages underneath. The presents will come later, when the weather gets more comfortable for shopping.

The photograph of the girls will be for our annual Christmas card. Allowing a couple of weeks for manufacture of the cards, another week to address them and a week in the mail, our friends should be getting our holiday greetings sometime early the first week of February. February is a nice month to be remembered. It is the time of winter when the life force is low. The joy of December has been forgotten. Spring still is too far ahead to be imagined. People tend to get stir crazy and send away in the mail for cruise brochures and seed catalogs.

It is nice to imagine folks coming home frozen and miserable from some errand, looking in the mailbox, and finding among all that trash mail a picture of our daughters grinning and wishing them a merry Christmas. The card will have the eerie immediacy of a time capsule.

"What's that?" they'll ask each other.

"It's a Christmas card."

"Maybe it's an Easter card."

"No, it's a Christmas card. You can see the tree in the background."

"That's not much of a tree."

"Well, the selection gets kind of thin along in January."

"It looks like a tree you'd find out at the curb the first Monday after New Year's."

"Don't be mean."

"Who's mean? All I'm saying is if I had a tree like that I wouldn't send out pictures of it."

"The picture is of the girls."

"How old are they?"

"They look maybe 11 and 12."

"That's in the picture. But I wonder how old they *really* are. In college, maybe? Married, with kids?"

"There's no telling."

"You know, that family has always seemed to me pretty disorganized. I heard once he didn't own a lawn mower."

"You're kidding!"

"Or a root feeder. And have you noticed they don't even have plastic slipcovers on their good chairs?"

"Well, I don't care. I'm putting them back on our list."

"I didn't know they were off."

"Every Christmas, when we don't get a card, I scratch them off. Then every February I put them back on again."

Christmas, as we see it, ought to be more than just another hectic deadline to be met. Christmas should be a durable state of mind. Travel with the herd and you're lost in the shuffle. March to your own drummer and people will be pleased to be remembered, even late. Unless love in February has somehow gone out of style.

28. A Miracle Recovery

We learn by doing. Yesterday I stayed home sick from work. It was a mistake I hope never to repeat. Henceforth, provided my legs can support me, I will appear at the office and make a pallet, if necessary, on the floor beside my desk.

Yesterday's indisposition was minor, and that was a piece of luck. Considering how strenuous it is to stay home sick, anything worse than a head cold might have been terminal. The children were out of school for the holidays. Freedom had sharpened their appetites. They wanted breakfast. Almost immediately, then, they would want lunch. After that it was likely that they would need transportation to somewhere.

I rose from bed, weakened and pathetic, and inquired in a thin voice how my wife would manage all these claims upon her along with the tragic burden of my illness. But she considered me no burden at all. In fact, on learning that I would be at home, she had immediately rearranged her day—scheduling business appointments and distant errands. She might be back briefly for lunch, she said. Then again, she might not. She is a woman with responsibilities of her own, my wife, engaged in the world. And of course I fully approve of that, even though I am mystified that her life cannot be arranged to accommodate my needs for comfort and convalescence.

Anyhow, I dressed, which I had not meant to do. And cooked for others a breakfast rather nicer than the one I'd thought might have been presented to me on a tray. The new snow had made the street treacherous. A neighbor's car turned sideways and lodged against the curb. I put on boots and went outside to aid in freeing the machine. Then it was lunch time.

I spread a table for the children. Nothing elaborate—liverwurst and cheese, soup and carrot sticks. (As for myself, I had no chance to eat, and anyway forgot to. Feed a cold? Hah! *When* feed a cold?) Briefly, then, their mother did appear. But only to take nourishment between appointments and to remind me of some place the girls needed shortly to be delivered to. Boots on again. Out to the cold car and the slick streets. Supper already bearing down. Back to the house. The dogs and the cats standing before their food dishes with a surly look. All fed, at last; all transported.

Alone, finally. But not with any thought of lying down and healing. Alone only the better to answer the phone and to concentrate on writing down messages for the absent. Still with rubber boots on, naturally — awaiting further commands.

I see now the homemaker's dilemma, and it is serious. Lives expand to fill the vessel that contains them. If you are the vessel, it's you who gets filled up, with no space left for your own needs, no time for your wants, no notice of your own infirmities. For a time that may work—for years, even. Then the overloaded vessel cracks and comes apart. And the homemaker scribbles a raging note, draws out the savings account and goes off to live in sin with a Berber scissors-grinder in Marrakech.

I have come back, instead, to the office. My intention is never to miss another day. Sometime I may get sick again. But except by my grayness of complexion and the absence of a pulse, no one will ever know it.

29. *All the Beds Are Full*

It is appalling, the way we sleep. And a few days' absence from home has worsened the shame of it. Do not try to tell me we were not missed. When we turned the car into the drive and opened the house door, the cats were waiting in a line, squinty-eyed with reproach. The old dog, home from having her teeth cleaned, followed us from room to room, grinning whitely.

A friend has given me a book, one chapter of which I try to read each night before retiring. Last night I put a page marker in the book and, as I got up from the chair and reached for the switch of the lamp, I looked for my wife in the bed. I could not find her. The bed was covered with animals—two cats at the head of it, two more in the middle, the dog sprawled grinning across the bottom.

Finally I spied my wife among them—just one of the tangle. And the years raced ahead in my mind, to that time when the children will be gone and the insurance on me will have been collected and she will be alone in the house. But not alone, really. Hardly alone! More cats and dogs will have come to lodge there. Through doors and windows left carelessly ajar they will wander in and out, unnamed and uninvited, bringing friends to stay the nights. She will mean to have them neutered—will fully intend to do that, but will forget. They will bear their careless litters in closets and behind the sofas and in the dark, untamed region of the basement. Their numbers will increase geometrically.

Strange tales will begin to circulate about the house and its thousand occupants. Neighborhood children, passing down the walk at night, will whisper among themselves and cross shuddering to the far side of the street. Repairmen will refuse to answer calls there. The postman will not ring twice, or even once; he will apply for a change of routes. Meters will go unread and the lawn uncut.

Neighbors will telephone the city with complaints. But city inspections being what they are, the inspectors may drive once quickly down the block, then caucus at their saloon of choice to gnaw pigs' feet and speak of depravity. And nothing will come of it.

She will, my wife, be like one of those fabulous crazed dowagers of the East—distant kin of a family of once-respected name but vanished means—dreaming away her last years in a cattery, surrounded by her trinkets and memories and by more love than is legal or sanitary. *Avant-garde* cinematographers will come to document the amazing spectacle of ruin. But the film, though eloquent, will be deemed unfit for public viewing. The presentiment of all this came powerfully to me as I searched her out last night among the varicolored heaps of fur on what, a long time ago, used to be our connubial bed.

"The animals seem glad to have us back," I said. "But where's a place for me?"

She smiled a little smile from the edge of sleep. The cats turned their green eyes upon me, level and defiant. The dog drew back her lips again and whitely grinned. And I returned to the chair to read another chapter in the book and wait my chance.

30. *The Museum Tree*

This year the tree went up without catastrophe. Late, of course, but uneventfully. The cats did not molest it. The single problem was the ornaments, of which there were too many.

Some of them we inherited from the years and the homes of our childhoods, found in the boxes where they were packed by other hands. Some we bought in a Mexican market in the first weeks of our marriage—small, strangely shaped animals, painted in dusty pastels. Some have been given to us by friends as remembrances of Christmases past and of shared times. And others our daughters have made. These last can roughly be dated by the skill of their manufacture. Enthusiasm begat dexterity, which later became form and delicacy, which begat finally something approaching art. All the ages of the children's growing are represented on the tree.

But the problem is in numbers. We began, as I remember, with two boxes. Now there are four or five, and the boxes have gotten larger. The cartons come up from the basement and always I suggest that for reason's sake, for the tree's sake, the ornaments will have to be culled. Every year I suggest that. And the whoops of outrage and denunciation are deafening.

Nothing can be cast aside. Not one item can be retired. The very mention of it gives to each of those things in the boxes—worn as some of them may be, frayed by generations of cats' claws, misshapen almost past recognition—a value beyond imagining. If broken, it must be mended. If faded, the tree's lights will color it. If merely hideous, it must be hung at the front, on a prominent branch, where its very outlandishness may prove endearing. The tree groans

71

and splays under the load. I groan. But quick hands keep finding and passing new icons to be hung.

I go into the houses of other, more tasteful people and I cannot help admiring the subtlety, the fine understatment of the Yule decor. Their trees are specimens of perfect symmetry, long-needled and statuesque. Displayed upon them might be one strand of tiny white bulbs, six blown-glass balls of translucent blue, a single ceramic dove. The impression is, at once, of extravagance and immense restraint.

The impression our tree gives is of overwhelming *fatness*. You would not guess it to be something that ever grew. It has a look of incredible but ruined complexity, like some fabulous machine that has been destroyed in an accident and partly reassembled.

Each year the ritual is the same. The ornamentation complete at last, we turn out the other lights of the room and sing together a song to the excellence of our tree. Even as the music rises, I know that next year the stack of boxes will be greater, the task more hopeless, the result more bizarre. Eventually, I suppose, we will have no choice but to add a second tree. Or to expand our activities to the barren oaks and maples of the outer yard.

But my protests are halfhearted in the end. For the point of what we do is not artistic but archaeological.

The ornaments are artifacts. Displayed there all together, like bones and shards in a midden, they amount to a jumbled chronology of lives—our own and many others. By their excessiveness, they confess no worse sins than hoarded memories and tender hearts. And those may be pardonable in the spirit of the season.

31. *Forever at Risk*

Somewhere on an icy highway in that small hour of morning a bus was lumbering ahead through curtains of wind-driven snow, bringing children home. Its riders, content to be in someone else's hands—the driver's hands—were mindless of the road. They slept or talked, played music on the radios and tape machines they carried. Crossing several hours of winter is, at that age, no worse than traversing any other span of time. The whitening world slips past the dark window. Presently the machine delivers you to where you're supposed to be.

At the road's other end, in unlighted cars with engines and heaters running, other people waited, peering at their watches. They were awake as night crossed over into morning. These were the parents—reasonable people and not given to outlandish fears. But just the smallest little ice-worm of concern worked inside them.

What followed was uneventful. Late by something like an hour, the bus arrived. The children stumbled off it, carrying their coats and travel kits. They'd gone to cheer their school team when it played in another city. Getting there and back had taken all day and part of the next. Debarking, some were drugged with tiredness and other were hysterical with it, depending on their natures. The driver wore the expression of a lifer just paroled. Whether that was from the journey or his cargo was impossible to know.

The waiting cars started up. Others swung in off the street onto the school drive, slipping and slewing a little on the bad footing. The children all were loaded. The bus driver guided his behemoth off to somewhere. The last light was extinguished in the school. The drive was empty and dark again, as if no one ever had been there.

At home, the young travelers lay directly down and slept. For those who'd waited their coming, sleep was less easy a gift. And there's the difference of faith and age—the difference between that time of life when everything, or almost everything, can be counted on to turn out fine, and that later time when you have known too well too many shattered survivors to be able to believe again that anyone ever really is safe.

How much of the danger—real and present—is a consequence of these complicated times? A plane bound for one place flies to another instead, directed by lunatics with grenades. Maybe those aboard are spared, or maybe not. Someone shambles raving through a shopping mall or fast food restaurant, emptying and reloading the gun, harvesting the innocent. Where is the sense in any of it?

But, then, when was there ever any sense? A wildfire drops its wind-borne spark on the cedar roof of a settler cabin and, in the morning, there is only smoking ash where a family used to be. The volcano looses a wall of muck and a village vanishes without a trace. A young girl hides in an Amsterdam attic, writing a testament of love and courage that soon will be her only voice.

The truth is that there is no sense or safety. Never was and never will be, in this or any time. So that the passage through a life can only be bought by unending and intolerable acts of faith. It's a dark-of-the-night sort of reality, and one that always comes clearer while waiting for a bus than while riding one.

32. *Investing in a Song*

Chief among the things I would not like to be, and there are many, is a bird in winter—on any day of winter, but especially after the blizzard has passed and whitened all. Warm now inside my window, I watch them at the feeder. Their uncomplaining courage is a wonder, their society and its countless little protocols an endless fascination.

The first to appear on any frozen day is a single bold sparrow. There is no timidity in him. One moment the feeder is unoccupied, and that brittle outer world seems without a possibility of life. The next, he just materializes there—or, rather, *she* does—a sudden animate mote of dusky brown. And cocks a beady eye at the window, as much as to say, *You're inside, you and your infernal cats. And I'm outside, trying to make my way. And that's a workable arrangement, if not exactly a comfortable one.* Then makes a little bow, choosing from the pile a particular bright seed.

Other stirrings begin to be seen among the inner branches of the evergreens beside the drive. The sparrow's colleagues, and their cousins in size, the slate juncos, are leaving the twigs on which they fluffed and suffered through the night. (Does a bird imagine spring? If not, what else can redeem such pain?) By ones and twos they come to the feeder and also to the top of an old wood stove beside it, where, on the worst days, another pile of seeds and grain is offered. Soon there are more than 20 of the small birds, all cocking their heads and bowing over their meal in a most mannerly and deferential way.

A companionable scene it is. And then a cardinal joins them. His courtesy is exemplary. Waiting at the side until the others offer him a place, he selects one seed—just one—then flies away to somewhere. And having scouted the terrain and found it safe, sends back his hen to take her meal before returning finally to see if something might be left for him. Contrast the courtliness of the cardinal to the jabbering boorishness of jays—two of whom arrive now, issuing threats, striking out with dangerous beaks until the others all have been driven away and they have the stove and feeder to themselves. In their blue-chevroned uniforms, they are as full of swagger and self-importance as two sailors on shore leave. But it is the empty bluster of bullies without real courage.

Because let a squirrel come, as one soon does, and the jays are gone without a peep. It is possible, I know, to make or buy a bird feeder that can defeat the cleverest squirrel. I have seen those, and they are very wonderful, but we have not gone to the trouble or expense of having one. They offend fairness, those contraptions. They imply that a squirrel's hunger in a storm gnaws less, somehow, than the hunger of birds, and I am unconvinced of that. So long as our ability to buy seed exceeds the ability of squirrels to eat it, as is the case for a little while longer anyway, they will be allowed at the table despite their gluttony and rudeness.

This one fills himself—spends a quarter of an hour doing it. But doesn't leave. Remains there on the feeder, his tail curled up and spread warmly over his back, looking at the uneaten grain, wishing his appetite would return, saddened to be unable to finish what he'd begun. At last, though, he gives it up— bounds from the feeder to an evergreen, and up that to a corner of the roof, and thence from roof to wire and wire to post and post to tree. And the birds come back.

They are an eclectic flock—the small and meek, the strutting and the brassy. And by these repeated goings and comings they pass their wintry days. In the harsh economics of Nature, some of them will not last the season through. But others will. One amazing day their frozen agony will pass away, and the world outside the window will be transformed. From greening branch they will sing of the durability of birds—a song in which we will be enabled to feel some little sense of proprietorship.

In tending the feeder, we do not give charity. We only prudently invest.

33. *Kitten and Balloon*

It is a sunlit morning in the bedroom, and as I write this the gray kitten, Roosevelt, is playing with an inflated balloon. I expect you know the nature of kittens—feisty, inventive, unquenchably optimistic.

The brilliance of winter light falls in bars through the window, drawing sharp patterns on walls and floor. Past those and through them, large-eyed and untiring, Roosevelt pursues her pink balloon, pausing only to chew a string of glass beads, her other toy, or to investigate her tail.

But it is the balloon she prefers. It is of respectable size for an adversary, but altogether helpless. It tumbles away foolishly when batted. The balloon has a painted face, a laughing one, that is about as large as Roosevelt's own. The laugh remains, even when the kitten snatches up the balloon near its stem and carries it with her teeth—though the eventual result of that is easy enough to guess. She does not know the thing will sooner or later explode. Such an event is not in the limited range of her experience. Nor can she see, as I do, that inside the first balloon there is another, and inside that one perhaps another still. Not even I can see those faces, to know if they are laughing.

What Roosevelt cannot know, either—has no way of suspecting—is that within the hour she is to be put in a box and taken away to the veterinarian's for surgery. It will be an operation of the female sort, necessary if the cats of a household are not to increase their numbers exponentially. All the same, this experience ahead will be her first acquaintance with the unhappy fact of pain. To this moment she has known nothing except food and fondling and the nearness of children's noses. This afternoon she will discover there is more, and worse. She will be baffled by it. To the extent she is able to think in such terms, she may feel in some way betrayed.

I have been touched by this, watching her play here in the sun on the floor in the perfect trust of what is, in a sense, one of her last hours of kittenhood. Will she come back changed in ways never intended? Changed in heart? There is no helping that, I suppose. But somehow, observing Roosevelt and her pink balloon, I cannot put out of mind the odd notion that I am seeing a metaphor for all our lives.

Gently it begins, or usually so. Life shows a laughing face. Then, like the balloon, it explodes unaccountably at our touch and reveals another face— endlessly, one face inside the other, some smiling and some not. Perhaps a marriage ends, and in that unexplainable catastrophe a child's world is shattered and rearranged. And so through all our years: Careers blossoming and then, in some moment, gone wrong or shunted in a new direction; a friendship ended, but another gloriously made. Great losses and great gains. And all of it—the good as well as the capricious hurt— visited on us in a fashion we no more understand than the kitten, Roosevelt, understands the principle of balloons or the reason for the painful journey she is about to take.

Yet there happens a curious and touching thing. Between these events it becomes possible to remember how to trust again. Never quite as freely, it is true.

Never without a coin of caution in the shoe. But it does happen. Kittens manage it, and so, almost always, do we. Being able to imagine our tomorrows requires it.

34. *Flowers Out of Season*

In the dark of the year, which also can be a dark season of the heart, we have profited from a visitation of elves. They came in the night, as elves usually do, and laid the downstairs table for a festive breakfast.

They spread a flowered tablecloth, then searched until they found the brightest yellow place mats, and arranged on those the company china. And on the chance these happy preparations might somehow have gone unnoticed, they also left a message. *"The Eleves,"* it said, *"were here!"* They have, these elves, a better eye for decoration than for spelling—but that is of no importance.

All this happened while we were sleeping. So that in the morning, when we went down the stair, we found the breakfast room transformed. That blossoming of flowers, that explosion of color, had swept the season's grayness quite away. And in that instant—not a bit too soon for our spirits' sake—thoughts turned from the cheerless march through winter to the expectation, suddenly made close and keen, of an easier and brighter time.

Much is said about the nurturing skills of parents. But I have been struck sometimes by children's innate sensitivity to our needs and to the nuances of mood around them. Their accomplishments of reason may be less. Logic does not confound them. Being animals in nature, their antennae are acute, and like the dog that

79

trembles on a cloudless day they sense the storm before it comes.

Just what the crisis in the household was—what impending storm of the spirit—I have forgotten. Nothing specific, I expect. Likely we all had been too long indoors, our temperaments drawn thin by too much cold and too much talk of politics and the economy and Iran and all the other craziness abroad in the world. Conversations moved in circles and ended with sighs. Food had become tasteless, friends occupied, work a tedium. In our war against winter's darkness, the dark had won.

The elves were not entirely selfless in their errand. They had in mind the ritual breakfast—French toast, sausage, the full production. And they sensed that strong measures would be needed to rouse the listless keepers of the house to such exertions. But whatever the reason, the effect was immediate and great. The sunlight falling through the window on that flowered cloth seemed unaccountably less cold. And then the weather did in fact change, breathing a balmy foretaste of winter's end.

Suddenly I began noticing seed packets on the racks in stores. And I began thinking of yard work—with distaste, of course, but at least thinking of it. Whatever had oppressed us passed from mind and even out of memory. Laughter reclaimed its place among the noises of the house.

It is the lot of parents to be awake at many strange hours, exchanging quarters for shed teeth under pillows, gnawing the carrots left for the Easter rabbit, drinking Santa's glass of milk with queasy stomach and doing the duties of elves in other seasons. But we have been shown that all this nurturing is not one-sided. For, thanks to those smaller elves of ours, we are certain now to make it through the dark tunnel of another month or two, our way lighted by that bouquet arranged for us in the creeping stillness of a winter night.

And that cloth will remain on the table until there are real flowers outside the window to take its place.

35. *The World's 12th Tongue*

The sweetness of childhood, my daughter has decided, is a myth. What has borne her under in anxiety and despair is her apparent inability to learn to speak the language of the French.

Let me say that I do not count this an important defect. I have tried to console her by supplying some historical perspective. For example, French was widely spoken in the court of Peter the Great and among the aristocrats of Czarist Russia. In the long run, what did that avail them? Since he was the king of France and advantaged by royal tutors, it may be supposed that Louis XVI also had an enviable mastery of the tongue. But on that winter day in 1793 when he was led to the Place de la Revolution and invited to lay his neck on the guillotine, the excellence of his conjugation of irregular verbs and his fluency in obscure tenses were no help at all.

In later times, the collaborators of the Vichy regime in World War II spoke French of an elegant sort. History has recorded what kind of men they were. Jean-Bedel Bokassa, who several years ago proclaimed himself the emperor of the Central African Republic, was a French-speaker of great accomplishment. He may even have used it when commanding the mass murders of school children and in the rituals of cannibalism he practiced behind the closed doors of his villa. And this very day, if you were to wander among the bomb craters and broken stones of what used to be the city of Beirut, you could be sure of hearing impeccable French spoken at almost every hand.

It is clear from the record, I tell my daughter, that fluency in the world's 12th ranking language (after Mandarin, Hindustani, Portuguese, Bengali and Malay, to name only a few) is no test either of character or of one's ability to get on in the world.

Most of the French literature worth reading already has been translated into English so as to reach an intelligent audience. The greatest French cuisine she will find beyond her means. The French manner is supercilious. French politics are inexplicable in any tongue. In short, apart from its occasional use in intimidating a haughty wine steward, the advantage of speaking French is unproved.

I have suggested to the teacher that my daughter's incapacity may be genetic, for I could not master the language, either, although, like her, I was commanded to. My ordeal was in college, where we all sat through the classes in a sweat of incomprehension, the sounds gibberish to our ears. On examination days, the room was alive with the rustle of papers being passed from hand to hand beneath the desks. After each test I had to throw away my shirt, whose inner cuffs had been transformed by use of a fine-pointed pen into lexicons of vocabulary and grammar.

I admit this without shame. It was necessary if we were ever to make it out of that place and get on with our lives. Which, without exception, we have done. Part of the process of becoming educated is to learn what, of all the body of information in the world, one doesn't need or care to know. One comes by that knowledge through painful exposures. And if one survives those, by whatever means, there will remain happy, wonderful years ahead for becoming sensible.

36. *The Bearable Mouse*

A winter mouse had invaded the cabin's back room and nested in a cushion. But there are worse perils than mice. Just up the road, our country neighbor's house had burned.

It happened two days before Christmas, and other neighbors told about it. Someone passing saw the fire. People gathered, wondering if the man who lived there still might be inside. but the house already was full of smoke and flame, and no one dared to enter. Old boards are wondrous fuel. They burn like gasoline. The people watched as the house became a flaming skeleton and then fell in upon itself. Then the rural fire company arrived. And after that the question of mortality was answered.

The man who lived there came riding in on his tractor from a back field, where he had gone with his dogs. He found a crowd standing round a square of smoking ash where his house had been. There was no insurance, folks reported afterward. He'd lost everything but the clothes he wore. And he wept at his ruin, they said—as who would not?

There was no sign of life about the place when we drove past in the car. Just the square of ash, gone cold and white. And I was sad to see it, because he was a good man and a good neighbor. I remembered a frozen March nearly 30 years ago when he and I spent a fortnight building fence together, cutting posts out of the woods and stretching wire to enclose what would one day be my fields and pastures. The weather that month was foul. Each morning before daylight I would wake cold in my cabin and go up to his house, the next one on our road, where we would sit at his table beside the stove and drink bitter coffee and screw up our courage for the day ahead.

Many of those days, sleet and freezing rain fell to ice our coats and gloves, and we had to make fires of gathered sticks to warm beside. But his ordeal was worse than mine, because I was a beginner at fence building, which is more complicated work than you might suppose.

From far down the line he'd wave to signal the wire was tight enough. And I, misunderstanding, would crank the ratchet of the stretcher one more notch. With a *whannng!* the wire would part, and I would see him leap aside to keep a quarter-mile of it from coiling back around him. Or, with the stretching safely done, we would work along the line stapling wire to posts. His hammer always struck the staple true. Mine sometimes hit a glancing blow and found the taut wire instead, with another unhappy result. His patience was amazing.

Until dark, we'd work. Then ride back across the fields together on his tractor and sit again at his table for a drink of something stronger than coffee to drive the ache and shudders from our bones. It was a hard two weeks, but satisfying. When we finished, my acres were safely enclosed. The fences still are there, built to last my lifetime. But now his house is gone.

I don't suppose I've ever spoken to my daughters about that work of a long time ago. For them, fences are just natural features of the land. But so was our neighbor's house—something that always had been there—and it shocked them to find it missing. We went back to the cabin, then, and made our supper and lay down in the dark, watching the flickers of light that the fire threw against our ceiling from the crack around the stove door. And the predations of the mouse in the cushion were entirely forgotten.

Among all the longer, surer dangers of impermanence, mice are the smallest worry.

37. *Forgiveness*

How much do animals know? How much do they remember?

With golden eyes as flat and cool as ice, he stared out through the wire of his kennel run at the stranger coming toward him through the snow.

For the first 15 months of life, the dog had had a regular home—a yard, his own food dish, a park for exercise, a rug indoors for inclement nights. Then, because of circumstances, he'd had to be boarded out, kenneled in a place with dozens or maybe hundreds of other dogs, a clamorous company, and given over to the occasional companionship of a different man.

What sense did he make of that? None, most likely. One morning he was loaded in the car, as so many happy times before. And after traveling a while, he was taken out and led past other boarders raging at their wires, and locked in an empty pen. And the car and man went unexplainably away. After that the other man, the new man, came weekly. And they would spend a day or two days looking for quail and pheasants together. Then he would go back to the pen.

Autumn turned to bitter winter. There was straw in his box, and maybe he slept warm, or maybe not. Certainly there was no rug on a heated floor. More than seven months he spent there. That was a third of his life—long enough you would think he might have forgotten all that went before. Now this stranger was walking toward his pen through the snow and, for a fact, in those flat golden eyes there was not a sign of recognition.

The man put down a hand. A nose was thrust cautiously toward it. There was a moment's uncertainty. Then dog face turned up—looked directly into man face. The yellow eyes were no longer cool,

85

detached. There was familiarity in them. They were full of things recalled.

He sleeps on the rug again, these awful nights. The old dog of the house, the one he used to devil so mercilessly, welcomes his company and is his friend, now that he's grown a bit beyond his puppy ways. And the cats? After all this time away, he still treats them as he first learned to, when they and he were all of a size—gently, a bit playfully and with profound respect.

What could he possibly understand of this strange experience? Nothing, I suppose, although surely he will remember it. Any creature that remembers home must also remember exile. Nor is he apt ever to forget that other man whose visits and excursions gave purpose to those weeks. What he does seem to understand is that the exile is over—not just interrupted, but really finished. Perfectly unperturbed now he sleeps on his rug, as if he'd never left it. When called to ride in the car, he goes gladly, expecting only good, never imagining he might again be left.

My explanation of all this would be lost on him, and anyway he does not seem to require one. Intuition tells him all he needs to know. He's home. He sleeps warm. And that's how it will always be. Some men learn about forgiveness by studying the lives of saints. And some of us keep dogs.

38. *My House of Many Waters*

The archaeologists of some future age will be amazed when their shovels lay bare the crumbled remains of the house I intend to build. *Whoever he was and whatever gods or devils he prayed to,* the good scientists will say to one another, *here lived a man of parts.* Because in my mansion there will be many rooms.

Self-aggrandizement and ostentation will not be its purpose, though. Looking closer, the archaeologists will notice a strange thing. Most of the rooms will be bathrooms. Probably they will draw from that all sorts of elaborate and wacky conclusions. They will postulate a culture scatalogically preoccupied. Or a civilization whose light flickered out ingloriously after a long pandemic of dysentery. Scholarly monographs will be published in support of one or another of these theses. Experts will line up for and against the scenario of terminal flux. Theologians may even become involved.

They will be dead wrong. The truth of the matter, which is not really complicated at all, is that I mean to build such a house—a house with five bathrooms at a minimum and maybe six or seven—because I live in a family of three women. That is not a sexist observation. It is a statement of absolute fact. Three of them—one wife, two daughters, the daughters just entering now upon an age of exceeding concern about their grooming.

In the course of a year I come under much pressure to rise early on weekend mornings to go with them to church or to other events of indisputable benefit. Generally—and increasingly—I am unresponsive. I lie abed, pretending sleep or sickness. This is not because I take lightly the needs of my spirit. It is because, if I do happen to get up, I am soon made to feel a nuisance and an obstruction.

Just the other Sunday, for example, aflame with lovingkindness, I threw back the bedcovers and announced joyfully that I would appear with them at the early service. Did this inspire any happiness? Not that you could notice. A bathroom happened at that moment to be unoccupied, and I made the mistake of going in there. Even a backslider's teeth occasionally

C. W. Gusewelle

need brushing. Instantly a current of outrage and impatience spread through the house. Angry talk could be heard through the door.

He's in the bathroom! Oh, no, not now! Tell him to pass out the hair dryer. Ask him if the curler is plugged in. How long? How much longer?

I live for the hunting season. My wife is mystified by this passion. She wonders where I find the stamina to rise morning after morning, in the smallest hours, to go afield after creatures I seldom catch. Actually, I don't care that much for hunting. But if you consistently get out of bed and dress at half past 3 o'clock sooner or later you are going to find a bathroom free. As I see it, the choice is either to be a hunter or live in a house next to an all-night filling station.

When the girls were small this was no burning issue. But now there is their hair. Soon there will be rouge and eye shadow to apply, toenails to paint and other, more arcane functions of adornment. So I total up our requirements. One bathroom for each of the females of the house, making three to start. My daughters have begun having friends in for the night. And the friends' hair is no less demanding of attention. Separate facilities will have to be provided for their morning convenience. Which puts us at five.

And what of the potted plants? There was a time when I naively thought that plants lived on window ledges and in hanging baskets. They do not—ours don't, at any rate. They spend a good part of their time draining in wash basins and bathtubs. That makes six. It might also happen that once in a while we would have an adult visitor. And I am not going to be put in the position of having to say that, although I am the owner of six bathrooms, none of them is available for the visitor's use. So the guest facility makes seven.

And if my own lamentable situation is to be in any way bettered—if I am to give up hunting and topping off my gas tank and making trips at strange times to 24-hour convenience stores—then the final installation will be mine. Bringing the grand total to eight bathrooms.

That is the central design feature around which the plan of my house will be made. We will be a happier family. Probably my health will improve. Those archaeologists of the future may make of it what they will. But if they themselves happen to be the fathers of daughters, it is possible that the cry of my great need will ring out to them from the mute dust and tumbled stones of another time.

39. *Defining the Turkey*

Our younger daughter has come of an age to have emphatic tastes of her own. Thus she denounced us at the table the other evening for placing before her something she refused to classify as real food. The offending object was a turkey roll, conveniently prepackaged in its own foil cooking vessel and bought from the freezer shelf at the grocery for a price only slightly less than that of precious metals.

She eyed the thing a moment with revulsion and naked contempt, then sank back in her chair and refused sustenance. We did not press her. Just then my own head was light and my tongue numb from several days of severe foodlessness. The diet I'm on is an extreme one—the one whose author was shot to death in a lovers' quarrel at nearly 70. My wife prescribes it from time to time, for my figure or whatever.

To me, that turkey roll looked exquisite. Small whining noises rose in my throat and my facial muscles jerked involuntarily as I contemplated it there on the platter. I did not mind that my daughter rejected it. Secretly I was pleased to see any of the competition withdraw. But I was curious all the same to know what it was about it she found so repellent.

"It's not real food," she said. "I like real food to eat—hot dogs and frozen pizzas and things like that."

"What the devil do you mean?" I demanded to know. "It's turkey. You always like turkey. You knew we were having turkey."

"It's not *real*," she insisted scornfully, as if that much ought to be self-evident. She stuck to her position and could not be moved.

Presently the facts came out. A real turkey has legs and wings. It has bones to give it definition. It is not bred to the shape of the pan. Plainly this monstrosity before her was not a turkey. Or if it ever had been, something unnatural had been done to it. She would suffer not one bite to pass her lips. She sulked. As I say, we did not oblige her to eat. Her mother ate, though. And so did I—heartily, with appreciative smackings of the lips and now and then a stifled sob of bliss at being allowed to break the fast. Her sister had gone elsewhere for dinner. But had she been there, you may be sure she would have eaten, too.

In the end, these coarse displays were more telling than any argument. She stole a taste while we pretended not to look. And then another. Except aesthetically, the thing was not so bad. The look of it still was wrong—unpardonably wrong. But the flavor was familiar. She decided she would accept nourishment, after all.

I sensed in this a valuable lesson for dealing with a daughter of distinct preferences and a rigid will. Threats and ultimatums are not the way.

She is, even at this age a comely child. It will not be much longer before oafish boys with racing bikes and pompadours will be seen loitering in the yard. And soon after that—by the time she's no more than 25 or 30—I probably will condescend to drive her and one or another of those louts to the movies together in my car.

Some of those ardent callers I will find more objectionable than others. But will I rage and issue commands? Not a bit of it! In a civil but effective way, I will simply make my position clear and without further comment withold her 50-cent weekly allowance. And sooner or later, I have no doubt, she and I will come to agree on what is a turkey and what is not.

40. *Spring Remembered*

Outside my window a tree is budded.

There is no explaining it. But neither is there any mistaking what meets the eye. The tree, a soft maple, has begun to reach in ancient faith toward a season that we cannot yet see.

The punishment of ice and polar nights is fresh in mind. Both my cars remain disabled by the freeze. The cats, whose habit it is to crouch waiting for the door to come ajar, have given up trying to get out. They did get out once, a week or so ago, and came back sooner than they'd planned, ears laid flat, looks of astonishment on their faces. And they have taken instead to sprawling on the tops of radiators.

It is the final heartless blast of a winter as fierce as any we have known. In the basement the old furnace throbs and rumbles. An arctic wind whines at the window corners. Birds hunker on the branch and the squirrels have resorted to eating roof shingles. Brief autumn is forgotten. The turn to a gentler season seems unimaginably remote. One foot set deliberately ahead of the last, like cattle plodding in blind file toward the comfort of a far-off barn, we march dutifully on but cannot notice the distance shortening at all.

Daily it does shorten, though. And there, outside the window, is the proof.

There is nothing about winter that any of us can usefully tell a tree. The tree—this one, or the one from whose seed it grew, or the one that struck its root in even colder earth—remembers them all. The hardest winters and the longest. The winters upon the edge of the vast, advancing ice; winters whose duration no calendar could measure. Winters that carved and forever changed the land. The memory of all that is written in the behavior of the descendant tree.

What it tells is that spring always comes, or always has. Not necessarily soon. But sometime—always. Against that certainty the tree prepares. Hence those out-of-season buds. A freezing rain has fallen overnight and, as I write this, ice sheathes every branch and twig. The buds are of a deep maroon color, and folded very tight, each the size of half a grain of popped corn. Unaffected by the cold, they wait their turn.

In winter's agony, the bird remembers the stirring bug, the greening seed.

The squirrel gnaws my bitter roof and imagines better fare.

The cattle plod grayly on, and so do we.

In all things alive, even in the hardest times, the tide of expectation is very patient, very strong.

41. How We Explain Ourselves

My fellow workers fairly often appear with their children in tow. I've done it and so have you, if you have youngsters. It happens in every office I've ever heard of, and is a ritual as obligatory as retirement parties and complaining about the lunchroom and flashing your teeth at the boss.

The newborn are brought in to be exhibited, either as proof of fecundity or for their inherent excellence, like prize smoked hams at a county fair. Leering faces bend over them. Clumsy hands pick them up. The place smells of machine oil and hot light bulbs and strangers. Growing sleepy, they scream. If babies remember the experience at all, it must be with confusion and disgust.

Visits in later years are for a different and more serious reason. They are part of every parent's endless and mostly useless attempts at self-explanation. We know from having been children ourselves once, and in a sad way strangers to our own parents, that nothing much can come of it. But one must try.

It's what I do. It's how we contrive to live. This is the place I disappear away to most mornings—where I spend half my waking hours, and more than half of yours. It's where I am when I'd rather we were playing in some park. There are friends here, and people who never will be. There's some satisfaction and some disappointment. In some odd way, I love this place and hate it at the same time. But I have to come here because it's the only work I know.

That's what we are hoping to communicate—some fuller description not only of ourselves but, at least in a preliminary way, of the prevailing adult condition, which has a lot in common with the condition of cornered rats. But it doesn't work.

I must have been taken to my father's place of work several dozen times as a boy. I remember that the building was very tall. And the elevator doors had elaborate engravings on them. And that he sat in an office with a lot of other people who seemed to like him, and probably one of the desks was his, though I could not tell which. I remember being made over by powdery-smelling women, so that even today the smell of talcum recalls the humiliation of it. What I never had was the slightest notion of what my father did. Later, when I was grown and myself employed, I met him there several times—a half-dozen, maybe—to go to lunch together. The talcumed ladies, older by then, still treated me like a little boy. And I was never really clear about his occupation.

Even knowing that, I have repeated the whole pitiful exercise with my own daughters. Or did, when they were smaller. They sat at vacant desks and I provided materials to draw with. Colleagues, in intended kindness, spoke of their resemblance to each other or to me. And news of this calamity struck them crimson and mute. I gave them coins, and they wandered off to other parts of the building and came back with things to eat.

Once, afterward, I heard them talking about it to a friend.

"He works in a place where there are pencils with good erasers and gum balls in a machine," they said. "He types."

It's as good a description as any.

42. *Two Times Ten Times . . .*

Put enough creatures under one roof—two-legged, four-legged, smooth-skinned and furred, all sharing the same space, the same beds, the same parasites and occasionally the same food—and the equilibrium gets delicate. But such a household, if that's what it can be called, is not assembled overnight. It happens insidiously, like the growth of the national debt. So that before the crisis is noticed, it already is past any hope of remedy.

The catastrophe begins modestly enough.

Two innocents stand before a minister and their lives are joined. The cat of one of them, and the dogs of the other, also are joined—noisily at first, but joined. And why not? Who would want to pass through lonely years and on into great age, bitter in the memory of a love fumbled away because of one misanthropic Persian shorthair and two arthritic beagles.

Children come. A larger house is needed. The cat expires, and afterward the beagles. The rooms seem empty without them, the family diminished. Replacements must be quickly found. But after that another cat appears on the lawn. And yet another, orphaned in an orchard, clambers into the basket of apples. All the rest move over to make room.

A winter storm drives a homeless hound to shelter on the step. Friends get a kitten, but find it neurotic and destructive. The painlessness of euthanasia is slyly mentioned. The others move over again, and that one brings to the mix his Prussian name and crazy inclinations.

Still, the man of the place is troubled at times by a sense of something lacking. What might it be? The man is a hunter. The cats are hunters, too, and gifted ones. But the game they wait for, owl-eyed, at a crevice in the basement is nothing fit for table. Children are a joy. They will comfort the man when the world turns cold. But that is for later. One has to live in the present, too. And children do not point birds. So that is what the man needs: A bird dog. He gives it as an early birthday present to himself. The beast's arrival inspires a lively yowling as the deck is reshuffled yet again.

In time, the house comes to seem smaller. Privacy is rare, loneliness impossible. One reaches for one's sandwich on the plate and finds it gone. A roast put out for thawing disappears. Blame cannot be assigned. The many eyes follow you guiltlessly, awaiting your next mistake.

I have been deliberately imprecise here about actual numbers. The law is meddlesome in that regard, and there is no point alarming the neighbors.

Some years ago a friend journeyed from a far city to stay the night with us. He made the mistake of leaving his bedroom door open, and appeared at breakfast haggard and amazed. It was, he said, like sleeping in Kruger National Park. He has been back once or twice since. But always with only enough time between planes to meet for a restaurant meal.

For the moment, now, our population is stable. But I am overwhelmed sometimes by the knowledge that, out there in the jungle of the streets, cats and dogs are multiplying tirelessly, and that in the inevitable course of things some of the results of those dalliances will find their way to us.

We are not just cranks. We are part of a vast and majestic process. And who can guess its end?

43. *Phil Never Makes Me Cry*

No man I know would submit willingly, regularly and at a fancy price to an ordeal almost sure to leave him emotionally shattered and sunk in humiliation. Which is why men cannot understand women's dealings with their hair-dressers. We are treading, here, on delicate terrain. But against the charge of sexism, as against the charge of libel, truth is the sovereign defense.

Men do not go to the barbershop to *find* themselves—to have their personalities revealed, as Michelangelo liberated the statue of David from its prison in a block of stone. They mean simply to get their hair cut. The preliminaries are few and to the point.

"Same way?"

"Yeah, the same."

"Kind of short in the back and full on the sides, right?"

"Right. Same way."

The matter is settled. Talk turns to more interesting things. The barber's chair is a pleasant interlude. One hears good jokes there, most of them unrepeatable here. Men are not vain about their hair. They ask only to be sent out in some presentable state, looking—for good or ill—about as they've always looked.

I enjoy my barber, Phil, a lot. He is a working man, like all the rest of us. He does an honest job for an honest dollar. He tells good stories. He is reported to be a powerful third baseman in the softball leagues, and I can say from experience that his tennis forehand is very strong. He does not, I am sure, regard himself as some kind of *artiste*. Or see my head as a blank canvas upon which to express the caprices of his imagination.

"About the same?" he says.

"The same," I reply. And we have a perfect understanding. His scissors go snickety-snick. He tells about having a run of luck at a blackjack table in Las Vegas. Maybe we make a tennis date.

"Next," he says.

And I go away content.

Not so the women of my house, or, I suspect, of yours. For them, the visit to the hair-dresser is an event freighted with danger and great suspense. They go there for adventure. Often as not, they come away in tears.

"Be honest," my daughter implored after a recent styling. "Does it look like me?"

"Sure," I answered honestly. "It looks like you with all your hair cut off. What happened? Did you go to sleep in the chair?"

"I told him what I wanted," she groaned. "But this is what he did."

"Did you pay him?"

"Yes," she said desolately. "A lot." And withdrew to the privacy of her room.

I have heard of certain very wealthy women who spend part of every day at the beauty salon. My heart goes out to them. That is more unhappiness than even the rich should have to bear.

Scientists pour their failed experiments down the drain. Hair stylists send theirs out to the dance. Phil, my barber, is a model of consistency. He may have booted a ball or two at third base, but in the shop he never has a bad day.

44. *Salvation's Ticking Clock*

Among my few virtues, promptness ranks foremost. It is the result, almost surely, of more than 30 years spent in an occupation governed by the clock. Journalists are obsessively devoted to deadlines, and in all that time I have never missed one. Although the fear of it is very great.

I cannot say what would happen to me—to my self-regard and my competence—if ever this rule were to be breached. But I suspect that punctuality in a journalist is a requirement of character as absolute as honesty in a bank clerk or chastity in a nun. And that if I were ever to deliver a story late—even once—that first small lapse would be followed by an appallingly rapid slide into dissolution and harlotry.

Now there are, I must admit, certain persons—more than a few of them—to whom this news of my promptness may come as a considerable surprise. The minister of the church, for one.

The first service of the morning begins at 9 o'clock. I imagine that other families make a point of arriving several minutes early and chatting companionably in the outer corridors before making their leisurely way to the pews. I only *imagine* this. I have never been there nearly in time actually to observe it.

Providentially, there is a side door through which the tardy may arrive, their entrance observed by not more than one-third of the assembled congregation. It is the only door I know. Yesterday our family slunk in at half past the hour, during the singing of the last hymn before the minister rose to speak.

A neighbor attends the same service, and from Sunday to Sunday it is touch and go which of us will be the last to be seated. Yesterday was no contest. Our neighbor was in his place and had gotten his wind

99

back and was looking straight ahead, like someone who might have been there overnight. Other communicants, being people of charitable heart, pretend not to notice. But I must believe that in some way these scandalous arrivals are being remembered and marked down against us.

What needs to be known is that in this, as in most else, I am blameless. I get out of bed when called. On Sundays I prepare the family's breakfast. I select a suit of clothes—the winter one or the summer one, depending on the season—and am standing beside the door, car keys in hand, at the proper hour.

But good example is useless. My wife is incapable of fast movement at that hour. When badgered about time she becomes flustered and resentful. Worse, my daughters have passed into that age where clothes and grooming are of great moment. From the upper reaches of the house can be heard the splashing of water and the slow purring of hair dryers and exclamations of dismay as various parts of intended costumes are found either to be in disharmony or in the laundry.

Time passes. You would not believe how *much* time passes.

The breakfast I have lovingly prepared grows cold. Milk curdles in the glasses. The eggs congeal. I get a book. Nearly all my reading is done while waiting to go to church. Over the years, if I had used that time to read theological tracts and explications, it would not have been necessary for me to go to church at all. I would already have been a very learned and possibly a very holy man.

We're doing the best we can! come the distant cries. And, sadly, that is true. *Get out our coats!*

The command about the coats makes my heart leap up. It suggests that we will be leaving that same day. Then the neighbor's car starts, and he drives hastily up the street and out of hearing in the direction of the church. And I know there is no hope of respectability left.

Someday, I am bound to think, my daughters will discover the function of clocks and the importance of timeliness to the pursuit of an orderly life. Before then, however, their career interest likely will have taken shape. And it will not, I pray, be an interest in the journalist's trade. I pray that most ernestly on Sunday mornings. Salvation being the work of a lifetime, the minister is necessarily a patient man. But I have known ministers and I have known managing editors. And the resemblance between them is not usually large.

45. A Passage in Sunlight

A child's growing up is observed not as a continuing process, but rather noticed in random, unexpected revelations. Always they touch the heart. Sometimes they almost take your breath.

This happened yesterday, the first sunny morning in memory. Light flooding through the curtains of her room had wakened her before the usual hour, and she was afoot in the house, startled by all that brightness, thinking school must have begun hours ago.

Those of us aged and seasoned to the tyranny of alarms are subject to no such confusions. The hateful instrument buzzes. We let go of dreams, leap up in numb obedience and set off running on the circles of our day. We may not understand the point of that—may not be able to say why or where we are running. But of one thing we always are sure: We know what time it is.

In fact, it was a few minutes after 6 o'clock, and already our morning ablutions were well advanced. My wife and I had spoken some small civilities, were mostly dressed, had consulted our lists and were exchanging information about our frenzied itineraries. Soon the water would be put on to boil. The dogs would be let out and the paper gotten in. The cats would present themselves to be fed. The plants would be watered, the window shutters thrown open to let in the day. And sometime after that, the children would be given advance warning of our intent to make them rise. All that is the routine. And it was while starting out on those errands of habit and duty that I met her in the hall.

I opened the bedroom door and there she stood, in her sleeping gown. And I leapt back a quick half-step, startled.

No one should have been there. Any children of mine still would be curled asleep, as they invariably were at that hour. What's more, this slender, stately creature was no child. Her eyes looked directly, levelly into mine—eyes so clear and deep that, for an instant, they struck me as helpless and speechless as a stone. The face faintly resembled one I'd seen somewhere, sometime. But who was she? What was she doing there?

For the least fraction of a second, I couldn't say. Then the odd moment passed. Of course I knew her; she was my own daughter—but grown almost into a young woman. How had it happened so suddenly, in a single night while we all slept? Or if more gradually than that, how had I not noticed?

"What time is it?" she wanted to know.

Not a child's words, those. So the clock finally has begun to rule her, after all, as it rules us all. What I wanted to say was, *No matter what the years bring, may you always greet your mornings with eyes like that.* Wanted to say it, but didn't. And the chance was lost.

My own voice came back then.

"Not late," I told her. "It's just the sunlight in your room."

46. On the Way to Other Country

They came to me foundlings out of the frozen woods of a lonely winter and we spent the next 14 years together, those little hounds and I. All of their lives and nearly a third of mine. As with any friends, it hurts very much still to think of them gone. I suppose in all that time I spoke more words to them than to anyone alive except my blood family.

We passed that first season together in the woods and they fed me—brought rabbits to the gun. Then we came to the city, which was perhaps the ruin of us all. They took distemper. I took malaise. We became citified, the prisoners respectively of wire fences and office walls, and it was all downhill from there.

One of the hounds, the one called Shorty, was outwardly phlegmatic and content. In his heart, though, he was insecure. He always sat very close. He groaned when you scratched his stomach.

The other, his brother, was the larger and more able and yet, somehow, never quite healthy. The distemper left him uncertain on trail, where once he'd been unfailing. But the hound's passion still was in him. And in later years, asleep on the rug at the foot of the bed, he would run and yelp in his dreams. I liked to imagine sometimes what country he was seeing, and whether he would ever see it again.

One autumn morning of his last year—he was alone by then—he slipped through a carelessly opened door and was gone for two days. Walking had become a labor, and yet somehow he traversed some 50 blocks of city streets and city traffic—ended up in the stairwell of a business in the industrial district, at a place where there were friendly hands and a can of dog food kept against just such an emergency. How he'd gotten there—more exactly, why he'd gone—remained a mystery. Maybe he was trying to make his way to open country again. Maybe by some instinct we know nothing about he understood that Shorty had gotten there before him.

That one's name was Slatz.

I buried them on a piece of wooded ground that as pups we used to run together, on a hillside sloping to a lake. The scene of many triumphs. And the other day, out walking, I came across the place for the first time in several years. Not quite by accident—nothing ever is entirely by accident. Moss of the woodland floor had crept up to cover the two piles of stones. The day was one of those on the dividing line between winter and spring ... sun and scudding clouds, still a little edge of March in the air. The trees were budded, the birdfoot violets just coming. I couldn't tell you how many exact such days those two and I had spent in that woods together. And for all the love that life has granted me, I felt lonelier then than in any time I readily remember.

One wall of the room in which I sometimes write— where I am writing this—is covered entirely with photographs.

Of a man I used to work for, and in whose home I spent many hours of boyhood. Gone now ... A scene from some battlefield of a generation ago, with Russian women bending over their dead in the rain and mud. All gone—gone even before I ever saw that photograph ... Of an old poet in Topeka, reading from his manuscript beside a window 30 years ago on one of the last summer afternoons of his life ... Of a friend in a duck blind, also gone. The blind and the man both ... Of other friends met in foreign countries, and still others moved away to distant states, unlikely ever to be seen again ... Of children grown beyond that moment, and almost unrecognizable in the pictures.

The two little hounds are there in one of the photographs, side by side in a brushy covert. Their heads are raised, their eyes fixed off alertly at some distant point from which a sound has come. They are very young and very eager. They know that life is sweet and they believe that there is nothing beyond that moment.

That is how I look, too, in the pictures on that wall. It is how all of us look—all of us arrested in time by the camera some years ago. For a hound, today is an eternity. Maybe, like them, we would do better never to consider the shortness of the race.

47. The Prisoner

The wonder happened unobserved. For more than a week the green chrysalis had hung attached to a withered sprig of dill, taped to the lower window shade of a room we rarely use. Inside that inch-long envelope, manufactured by a worm, a transformation was taking place.

Children know all about the changing of caterpillar into butterfly. Adults have spoken of it as truth, so the young accept it as just another fact in Nature—like talking parrots, the distance to the nearest star, the fabulous multiplying power of a single seed. One passes through a lifetime with that catalogued among other curious but perfectly common events. It happens the whole world over, millions—no, *billions*—of times in a single season. Somewhere at every hour of every day, safe to say, these metamorphoses are occurring in numbers beyond counting.

All this the rational mind understands and accepts. After that it is better not to think about the subject too much. Because someplace way beyond reason, at the level of daydreams and imagination, the process of a butterfly's becoming can produce—or does in me, still,

105

at this age—a breathless and almost giddy astonishment.

I meant for us to watch it together. Each day we inspected the chrysalis for some sign of stirring. We had been told that in the last hours before emergence its color would noticeably darken. If it did, we missed that—missed it all. It simply happened as most wonders do. One afternoon, when we went to check, the envelope hung empty from its sprig. And there, on the bookshelf below it, was the black swallowtail fully formed.

Someone has said, or I have read somewhere, that a butterfly does not realize it is capable of flight until it feels the stirring, lifting power of a breeze. In that sudden instant, the difference is complete. The thing that used to creep understands that it can ride the air. For many creatures, even sometimes for us, there are moments a bit like that in which, in a rush of unexpected recognitions, we feel our possibilities change. But nothing, I suppose, compared to what a new butterfly must experience upon the discovery of its wings.

For the one on our bookshelf, that never happened. In that closed and windless room, it never transcended the memory of its crawling former self. It never flew. Some days it perched on a round stone, picked up years ago in a forest and kept for a paperweight. Other times it crept up to the window and seemed to be looking out, its wings spread so that the light passing through the blue-black background and the smaller markings of yellow and orange was like sun through medieval colored glass.

At first, whenever we entered, it would give a small show of alarm, standing higher on its legs, drawing its wings together as if preparing for the escape it hadn't mastered. Later, it seemed to become more accustomed to us. One of the girls extended her hand, and the butterfly stepped onto her finger and clung there while she held it higher against the light. There was a brief discussion of setting it free outdoors. But we were pained to think of it becoming a bite for some passing bird.

"We'll keep it here," I said. "It seems content enough. And they only live a few days, anyway." Someone raised the question of what it would eat. "They don't eat," I answered, with the typical certainty of the uninformed. "They only eat when they're caterpillars."

Days passed. A week, and more. The swallowtail climbed less often to the pane, spent most of the time on its stone or beside it, moved only slightly when we came near. Yesterday, I found it on the window sill—still beautiful and undamaged, but lifeless, having as its final act spread its wings out perfectly flat as if in a collector's display.

Too late, I troubled myself to do some reading in a book. Not only had there been no breeze in the room. There'd been no nectar, or even any water. Butterflies, I learned, do feed and drink. Why else, in the wild, would they travel as they do from flower to flower. By our concern, it had been kept from being all it might have been. And then, in ignorance, I had starved it.

In the face of the truly miraculous, how clumsy we usually are!

48. Hit and Run

My daughters have begun to speak of automobiles, and the future unfolds before me like a tormented dream.

Their need for cars is not immediate. Both still are years away from being allowed to drive. In this single area, at least, government and its laws are on my side. Already, however, the girls have started examining the machines of the road with slitted eyes, declaring their preferences.

Their taste, I find, runs to foreign sports models either of red or metallic silver color—wonders of engineering, available at a price only slightly larger than my annual wage. "Yes," I say, when one of those is pointed out to me. "That's a whiz of a car, all right."

"Isn't it cute?"

"Right. Cute." If I seem not to have much heart for the discussion, it is because my own car—in which I am driving them to some place of their many amusements—has 130,000 miles on its odometer, and I am listening with a thrill of anticipation for the noise that will announce the failure of its next major part.

"I don't need one yet, of course."

"Of course," I say.

"But you'll think about it?"

"Right. I'll keep it in mind."

That is how the conversations end now, inconclusively. But the time will come when the discussion will be pressed to its finish. Meaning that I will be reviled as a fascist and bad provider, or else I will find myself fidgeting in a chair before some banker's desk. It used to be held that every child deserved a loving home, a change of underclothing, three meals a day and a clean bed. In the short span of my own lifetime, the minimum entitlements of childhood have been expanded to include guitar lessons, several thousand dollars in orthodontics and a foreign car.

Friends who began their families earlier already have passed through this crisis, taking title to an impressive number of machines and getting to know body-and-fender men on an intimate basis. The stories they tell are like the stories men bring back from war.

Youngsters of my generation did not have their own cars. Being cruelly deprived, we had to wreck our parents' cars, which we did often and expensively. For many years, my father worked at two jobs—one during the daytime, another at night. There were times in adolescence when I resented seeing him so seldom. Now I understand that he was not propelled by greed or ambition, but by the need to fix up his one automobile so that I might take it out and turn it over again. Always, when he handed me the keys, it was with the sadness of a man who expected soon to be afoot.

Barring an unforeseen inheritance—unlikely, since I am the oldest of my line—silver sports cars are out of the question. Derelict Jeeps occasionally are offered for sale by some agency of the government. Their steering wheels often are on the wrong side, which gives a certain foreign flavor. And there is a pickup truck sitting in the weeds of a farm I know, which might, with the investment of a few dollars, be persuaded to run again.

Sometimes, when my attention is directed to a sleek example of alien craftsmanship, I reply by mentioning these humbler possibilities. A shadow passes across the sun. The atmosphere turns suddenly chill, and my daughters draw as far away from me as possible on the car seat.

"But that truck's a whiz," I tell them. "Why, it's a genuine antique."

They look straight ahead at the road, their faces grim.

"It's one of a kind," I say, pressing my advantage.

"Look," they say then, coldly. *"Forget it. Let's just drop the subject of cars. Okay?"* And, reluctantly, I do. But I am sensible enough not to mistake these preliminary skirmishes for the war itself.

49. *A Forgotten Art*

I would give a lot just once—just once again—to sleep the way an adolescent sleeps, or an old dog dreaming on the warm flagstones of an afternoon in spring. They have that in common, children and old dogs do, being creatures in the season of their satisfaction. They lie down somewhere, anywhere. They arrange themselves a moment. Then effortlessly, guiltlessly, they let sweet mindlessness claim them.

They dream, I think—am sure of that, in fact. Old dogs yelp and move their legs as some deep memory carries them again across known country. The child speaks out from darkness a disconnected word. But these dream events are small and mostly gentle. The sleeper does not wake. Hours pass; whole days might almost pass, it seems. That complete is the abandonment to the easy dark.

In boyhood I had a friend who could remain asleep as long as luck allowed. Awake, he was perfectly healthy and energetic. But that was not the condition he preferred. Some weekends he hardly left his bed. Call him up in mid-afternoon on a Saturday, and the phone might as well have been ringing in an Egyptian tomb. There was that much hope of an answer.

Abstractly I remember sleep like that—the idea of it, although not the feeling, not the actual sensation of it. It has been too long ago. Adolescents and old dogs have a talent for it, almost never found in old men and pups. Oh, we lie down at night, the pup and I—one of us on the bed, the other on the rug at the foot. The light is turned out, and I experience what passes for rest. But there is no far remove. Even in those few still hours a clock is ticking in my head. And in the heart, anxieties are ticking.

Events of the day are reviewed, the crowded march of them impossible to halt. Difficulties of the morrow multiply. The mind's eye never quite closes. The mind's ear listens for a stealthy hand on the doorlatch. If there happens to be a dream at all, it is literal and dull, so true to life as hardly to be worth remembering. Unless I have damaged myself by some foolishness the night before, that's how it always is.

Then, alarm or no alarm, it is habit's fixed hour for rising, give or take five minutes either way. And sitting on the bed's edge, I feel not noticeably different awake than I felt asleep, or before I lay down. At just that instant, or sometimes a bit before, the pup also rises to begin his day. He has not learned to sleep yet, and I have forgotten how. Our circadian tides thus rise and fall in almost perfect synchrony, although for him, with time, the condition will be correctable.

He goes out the back door to his errand in the yard. I go out the front one for the paper. The kettle whistles. The day's war is joined. Passing by the children's rooms, I still detect no sign of stirring. The empty husks are there under the covers, but the living parts of them have sunk far down and away to a distant, perfectly untroubled place.

Just one more time to sleep like that, I think. And then—is it obligation, or is it envy?—I lay hand on shoulder to draw them back from where they've been. Back from that region where age forbids me to follow and which, in the natural course of things, they'll soon enough forget how to enter. Childhood being short, I'd rather end up an old dog than an old man any day.

50. *Accidental Wounds*

The intention had been to spare them hurt. To that end I had years ago invented a gentle fiction. But things do not always work out as we mean them to. And so, on a recent sun-washed day of spring, I found how clumsily I'd made the hurting worse.

It began with the smallest question.

We had seized the sparkling weekend, my two daughters and I, to make a beginning on a long-planned project in the woods. The exact nature of the task is unimportant. But it involved hard working with our hands—the three of us together. And now, at midday, in a perfect state of comfort with the sun warm overhead and the breeze April-cool on our faces, we sat on mossy stones, listening to bird songs and sharing our lunch from a sack.

"Where did you bury them?" the younger one suddenly asked. Not morbidly at all. Just wanting the information. And she spoke their names—the names of the first two dogs in her memory, and the greatest ones in mine. The two little rabbit hounds, dead these many years.

"Over there," I said, and pointed. We looked together across the glitter of the pond. "Up on the hillside there. It was a favorite place of theirs."

"And where are they now?"

The question had been asked before. And again I spoke the fiction which, through usage, had come to be expected.

"Running somewhere, I suppose."

"Oh," she said. Reassured by the telling of it, she and her sister turned their attention back to lunch.

The day moved on. The afternoon light softened and the breeze fell. Woodpeckers sent their urgent rappings across the stillness. Small fish rising made circles on the dark water. We had finished our work—or that part of it we had set for ourselves. But we were together in a flawless hour, and to leave quite yet was unimaginable. So we contrived a make-work task, carrying and placing flat stones for a path across the shallow outlet of the pond.

We were some yards apart when I heard a sharp, happy cry. It was the younger one again.

"I saw a dog," she announced to us. "There, through the trees." Her face was turned toward the hillside.

"Just one?" her sister asked.

"It might have been two." She meant to be truthful, but hope was remaking the truth in her mind. "I'm pretty sure it was two!"

"Do you think it could be them?" her sister asked. Older—but in some ways a child still. My daughters were looking at me.

"Could be," I said—and wanted those words back immediately. Knew the cruelty of my mistake. The younger one started away up the hill, then. Excitement chimed in her voice. Excitement and unreasoning faith. She was calling them by name.

"They can't hear you," I said. But she went on a little way in spite of that, unwilling to believe. The older one and I walked back together along the pond dam to the dock, where she lay down on her stomach, staring into the black water.

"Why didn't *you* call them?" she asked finally. She put it as a question. In those few minutes, though, she had come far toward puzzling out the answer for herself. It was a while before I could reply.

"Because," I told her then—the truth at last. "There'd only be heartache in it."

She didn't speak or make another sound aloud. Just lay there, face down toward the pond, her tears sending out silent rings where they struck. The other one was coming back through the trees, now, and would also shortly understand, if she did not already. The fiction meant in kindness had gotten out of hand,

113

had been exposed. And instead of sparing them grief it had caused them to live it twice.

51. *Daddy's Secret Shame*

The family was jostling and elbowing around the dining room table for the opening of the mail, which is the big moment of our day.

Breakfasts we rarely get. Lunches we take somewhere else. Suppers are chaotic and hasty affairs. But mail time brings us close, all snatching at once for the envelopes in the unworthy suspicion that one of us might claim a piece of correspondence intended for one of the others.

My preference would be to take charge personally of this operation, to sort and distribute the mail myself as an expression of my power as nominal head of household. But they won't let me. The postman's arrival is announced by the dog, raging and frothing at the door. I rush quickly out to the box on the side driveway in hope of looking through the stack without interference. But it's no use. The others have been alerted, too, and are waiting, steely eyed, at the table.

Yesterday my wife and daughters were richly blessed. Only one envelope was for me. It was a slick, fat envelope, and I turned it importantly in my hands before breaking the seal.

"What's that?" one of the girls asked.

"How would I know?" I told her. "Can't I even look at my own mail in privacy?" I took out the brochure, illustrated in color. "It's some kind of special offer," I said.

What the brochure was offering, at a ridiculously low price, was 12 hours of hard-core pornography on video

114

cassettes. That's how it described the merchandise. *Hard Core* may even have been the name of the company. Each of the one-hour tapes was listed by title, with a lascivious illustration and excerpts of reviews by the important New York porn critics.

I tried to wad the brochure back into the envelope.

"You ordered *that?*" my daughter asked, amazed.

"Of course I didn't order it. It's just junk mail for Occupant."

"It doesn't say *Occupant*." She pointed to the address on the envelope. "It says you. They even spelled it right."

"Well, I didn't send for it. Obviously this scummy outfit bought a mailing list from someone."

"Sure," she said.

"Listen, once you're in somebody's computer you are fair game. They buy and sell you like bacon. It's the new form of white slavery."

"Whose computer are you in?"

"Three credit card companies," I told her. "Two insurance companies. Four banks. An oil company. One stock brokerage. My employer. The IRS. And the church. I think the church has a computer."

"Would the church sell you to Hard Core?"

"I doubt it. The stock broker I'm not so sure about."

"Anyone else?" she said. "Think. Have you ordered anything by mail?"

"Bulbs," I said. "I sent away for some tulip bulbs for your mother."

"From where?"

"Holland. All bulbs come from Holland."

"Nobody's that naive," she said. "Amsterdam is the pornography capital of the world. Order tulip bulbs and you're asking for it."

"I am *too* that naive," I whined defensively. "How was I to know that Assorted Spring Colors meant Hard Core."

She curled her lip and went away muttering. "Now I understand," she told the dog, "why he's so funny about the mail."

52. *Fences Are for Jumping*

Some overpowering fascination lies outside the fence, and from time to time Rufus, the bird dog, goes out to seek it. The fence for him is not so much a confinement as a kind of theoretical suggestion of the boundaries he is expected to observe. Dutifully he marks the perimeter of his turf. And he barks inside the wire like any other dog—especially when he's glad to have it between him and whatever is passing on the other side.

But when the urge for wandering comes over him, and if he suspects no one is watching, he can levitate himself across it as lightly as a sparrow. And in an eye's blink he is gone.

It has led to some unseemly displays: Frantic foot races up the block, with me in pajamas at an unnatural hour of morning, stumbling through other people's flower beds and between the houses, bellowing his name under the bedroom windows of sleeping neighbors.

Once he was gone three days. I was out of town, but my wife notified all the proper agencies, then lettered a sign with his name, description and our phone number and tacked it up, with all the other sad bulletins, on a pole beside the street. Then, suddenly as he'd left, he floated back over the fence and reappeared, full of guilt and unspoken mystery.

It happened again one night not long ago. We let him out for a last patrol of the yard. Then something distracted us, and it was a while before we thought of him again. And when we did remember, I knew without looking that he'd have flown. I shook my daughter in her bed.

"Where's the dog?" I demanded to know.

"The *dog?*" She'd been asleep an hour and was confused. "I let him downstairs. You let him out."

"Well, he's gone," I said, accusingly. "Gone!" In a crisis caused by one's own stupidity, it always helps if you can find some innocent to blame.

We pulled on sweaters, my wife and I, and set out in the car. "He won't survive the morning rush hour," I told her.

"Drive slower," she said.

The headlights showed only empty streets, dark houses, empty lawns. After an hour of cruising, we gave it up. "If he's lost, he's lost," I said, in a voice that suggested *good riddance*. Because he was, in several ways, a hard dog to live with. But what I really was thinking was how uselessly, stupidly busy the previous autumn had been and how many hunting days we'd missed—penned up, both of us.

I went out a final time to look in the fenced yard, which of course was empty. From several houses away, I heard the sleepy barking of neighbor dogs—home bodies, respecters of the law. And just on a chance, I called once. A shadow separated from a bush. There was a flash of movement across the grass. And through the door came the truant in a rush.

He never apologizes afterward. He just arranges himself in his soft chair and looks at you with those flat, yellow eyes and wonders what you plan to do about it. Build the fence higher? Watch him closer? It doesn't matter. He is patient, and he knows one day you'll make another slip. Some spirits aren't for caging. Either you learn to live with that, and master your envy, or you get yourself a different kind of dog.

53. Bless You, Mr. MacArthur

All their friends, it seems, have summer jobs, raking in fortunes at the minimum wage. But timeliness is everything. And my daughters, entering late into the chase, do not find themselves swamped with career opportunities as ice cream dippers, strawberry slicers or passers of hamburgers across the counter. The price of a movie ticket being what it is, they see a season of poverty ahead and are depressed.

"I'll do *anything* for money," one of them said yesterday. I hope that is hyperbole.

Mowing yards is out. My position has nothing to do with sexism or the nature of the work, which is constructive and satisfying. But if they are going to cut off their toes they will have to do it on their own hospital policy, not mine. Baby-sitting is an option. In a month, at today's rates, an energetic sitter can earn double the annual per capita GNP in most Third World countries. The pickings are lean, though. The old standby babies have grown up, or interlopers have taken over the territory. The phone doesn't ring the way it used to, in the days before their great need and new-found ambition.

At their age, all catastrophes are final. They see themselves passing on into their twilight years— matrons of 18 or 20—still receiving an allowance that runs out on the fourth day of the month. Grades, good grooming, a pleasing manner . . . what good is any of it if it can't be translated into bringing home a little independent loot?

I know that rage to succeed. I had it once myself, though mercifully it passed. And I remember vividly the summer that it drove me off the porch swing and out into the real world to work for Mr. MacArthur. He was a wonderful man. How could a boy ever forget anyone that impressive and big-hearted?

He owned a hardware store, Mr. MacArthur did, on a street that had had a flood. I walked in his door and he hired me. Just like that! Some men, even then, were prepared to look beyond small size and stammering timidity and make a social investment in the young. The receding floodwaters had left the basement shin-deep in muck and full of overturned racks of Mr. MacArthur's damaged inventory, chiefly automobile mufflers and tailpipes and such, dusted over and pitted with orange rust.

Every morning, afire with ambition, I skipped down the stairs into that lightless pit—the basement wiring had been ruined, so there was no bulb—dragging stuff from the tangle and wiping the metal clean with oily rags. Mr. MacArthur stayed up above, waiting on customers or leaning back with his feet on his wooden desk, smoking short cigars. At noontime he would come to the top of the basement steps and call me up for my sandwich, beef with slices of pickle on it, which he brought from the deli down the street.

There was enough work in that basement to last a summer, he said. And my heart was full of gratitude as the sandwich turned orange in my rusty hands. He started me out at 50 cents a day. Then, knowing quality when he saw it, raised me to 75. One evening, when he closed the store, I invited him home to meet my parents—I in my ruined clothes, he in his striped suit and vest. We sat on the porch and drank homemade strawberry ice cream floats, and my mother looked at him through eyes slitted with hate. But as far as I was concerned, nothing was too good for a man like Mr. MacArthur.

I was 12 years old, then. And any later successes have been built on the start he gave me. I couldn't imagine I'd ever work for anyone finer than that. And as it turns out, I haven't. So I tell this story to encourage my daughters in their predicament. Keep knocking on doors, I promise them, and your chance, too, will come.

54. I Think the Earth Moved

The old dog knows someday a storm will kill her. Each time she waits in wide-eyed terror, and wonders, *Is this the one?*

The other afternoon we found her pressed against a wall, her face thrust under the corner of a chest of drawers. Nothing could tempt her out from there—not rattle of food dish, nor calls to run in the yard. Perfectly still, she lay, and so rigid to the touch that we wondered for a moment if maybe the storm had taken her already. Except there *wasn't* any storm. The languid day was running on toward its end under a cloudless sky. No premonitory winds gusted through the pale new leaves. Afternoon deepened into tranquil evening.

But about this central matter of her destiny, the old dog is never wrong. Just before the last light went out, a bank of thunderheads rose up to southwest behind the trees, and then came striding in off the prairie, alive with electrical discharges and spilling a mutter of thunder.

She's not a coward by nature, the old dog. There's no fear of anything else in her. But when the storm-terror claims her she is awful to see. Her whiskered brows are drawn up in dire expectation and her eyes roll whitely in her head. Her sides heave with panting. Touch her anywhere, and you can feel the hammering of her heart. Sometimes she hoists herself into the bathtub and waits like someone put prematurely in a coffin. Other times she hurls herself at the door, howling and raging to be let out of the room. But let out to what? To another room, and another door. And finally, beyond the last door, is the night and the great noisy thing that has come hunting her. And surely she doesn't want out *there!*

She's a trial to be around at times like those. We care a lot for her, but there's hardly anything more troubling than to see a friend overcome by shuddering horror that can't be helped or even in any sensible way explained. A kind word, the touch of a caring hand, are meaningless. The storm has come for her. And there's no room for any other thought than that one.

Her final sanctuary is underneath the bed. But the bed is low, with not much space between springs and floor. Things are stored under it—picture frames and such. So it's not a crawlway easily gotten into. But fear can multiply strength tenfold.

"I think the earth just moved," I sometimes say to my wife in the middle of the night.

"Huh?" she says.

"The air is cool through the open window," I tell her, "and I can smell the wetness of the wet pine needles and truly, rabbit, thou must tell me, did the earth just move for thee as it did for me?" Sometimes I talk that way in the night if I have been reading the wrong kind of books.

"Don't be silly," she says. "It's just the old dog under the bed. There's been a thundershower. The earth stayed still. It was the dog and the bed that moved."

By morning we are restored to reason, the dog and I. She heaves and claws her way out from her hideaway. She breathes normally again, and her eyes are calm. But she knows that the storm will come again and one day it will kill her, and probably she is right. Her old heart will simply stop. And so, when I feel the earth move, may mine.

55. Covering Ground

On vacation, I am left unsatisfied by any day of travel that does not end with the parched throat and bone-weariness of a forced march. Only by the severity of the ordeal can I know for certain that I have gone somewhere.

Some people plan their journeys in scrupulous detail. They limit the number of miles they will travel each day to a sensible, a leisurely number. Each night's lodging along the way is chosen on account of some particular virtue. The hotel dining room is telephoned weeks in advance to learn what dessert *flambé* will be on the menu on the night in question. Inquiry is made as to the dimensions of the swimming pool and the availability of sauna baths. These travelers pass across the country in a civilized way, arriving well rested and assured of amenities.

Intermediate points do not interest me. My eye is fixed on destinations. I settle in the driver's seat, my hands lock in a death grip on the wheel and we strike forth cheerlessly upon the highway, embarked on a single-minded careen toward wherever it is we are finally bound.

Daybreak, if I have anything to say about it, finds us already briskly in motion. Except for stops for gasoline and carry-out boxes of greasy victuals, I do not mean for any of my passengers to set foot on earth again until the moon has ascended far up in the east, cries of lamentation have risen loudly in the rear seat and my own eyes have glassed over.

Where we might call the next night's halt is anybody's guess. Finding a room at nearly midnight along a major tourist route in peak season requires patience and resourcefulness. Our luck this trip has run to smallish motor courts operated by families of immigrant East Indians, located next to 24-hour restaurants with names like *EAT* and *Truckers Welcome*. There, under the naked bulb, while wife and children sink moaning into the sleep of drugged exhaustion, I consult the maps and lay plans for the next day's rampage across several states.

Scenery means almost nothing. Mountain ranges are traversed unseen in darkness, their majesty detectable only as a slight stuffiness in the ears. Our memories of various sectors of the continent are not of foliage or topography but of the comparative fastidiousness of public rest areas alongside the interstate highways. Tonight, for example, one of the children remarked we must be headed north because of the lesser number and smaller size of the bugs striking the windshield.

As I've said, not all people travel this way. But we do, and obviously we are not alone. Not many hours ago we pulled into a service station to fuel the car and ask advice on how to bypass the next city, avoiding the hazard of being distracted and delayed by some interesting sight to see.

A small boy was sitting on a chair in the station's office—a boy of 12 years, looking long-faced and bewildered. The lad was from somewhere in Illinois, the attendant said. His parents had stopped for gas. He had gone to use the rest room. His parents had finished gassing the car and had driven on without him. That had been 30 minutes or more ago. When the parents noticed he was missing, they would certainly come back. That is, if they could remember where they'd gotten fuel.

Now there is a family whose whole attention is concentrated, as mine has always been, on the real purpose of any journey, which is to click off the miles and get to the end of it. The episode of the forgotten child seems to have made a large impression on my daughters. They know my nature behind the wheel.

Very close together, very wide awake they sit in the rear seat. They do not ask the possibilities for dinner.

They do not inquire to know when we will call the night's halt—how soon, or in what town. And they do not speak of any need for comfort stops. Above all, not of those. However long until bed, they do not mean to leave the car again.

56. *Land of the Short Summer*

A single long day's drive has delivered us out of the suffocation of the plains and into a country of deep sky and pine-edged waters and three-blanket nights.

That is the wonder of residing not in some postage-stamp principality but in a continental nation. Oceans bound us. In brackish waters of the South, alligators sulk and dream their reptilian hunger among the drowned mazes of the mangrove roots. Mountains heave up their rocky spines and then, on their western flanks, sink away to sun-scalded desert. The prairie reaches northward to the start of these deepening woods. And so vast is the whole that no one of these— swamp, prairie, peak or forest—begins to describe it. They are only its incidental features.

Our family is together now, after half a summer spent largely apart. I was traveling on business. Our daughters were at camp. Their mother, in our absences, tended the weedy garden of all our affairs and kept life in its remembered shape. Last night, for the first time in many weeks, we were all under one roof.

We might have made a fire in the wood stove, but didn't. The hour of coming in from fishing was late. The blankets on the shelf against the log wall were many. And, anyway, it is fine, in the deep of July, to go to bed cold and feel the warmth arriving. Before sleeping, I went out barefoot on the grass at the lake's edge to watch the sky.

Here, where no other light intrudes, the stars are past numbering. The Aurora Borealis, the northern lights, were making a display, sending long bars of energy up from the horizon, faint in one moment, pulsing brighter the next. In more than 40 years of coming to this north country I've seen them so well only once before. And that was in my own boyhood, standing at the edge of this same water. The northern sky, the changeless country of these northern summers, express somehow the larger, longer calculations.

Enormous the land—vast its power and its possibilities. But the galaxy spins on across eternity. Terrible cool discharges of magnetic energy agitate the nights of a certain sector of an inconsequential planet. And does it matter a bit who is watching, if anyone is? Or in what year? Or from what political jurisdiction? Only to us, perhaps. And yet, in great ways and small, the pageant proceeds.

Yesterday, a pair of wild mallard ducks, traveling by foot from the pothole where they'd nested, stood their ground and stopped the car to get their clutch of fuzzy hatchlings across. Last night, among the reeds just past the boat dock—where starshine on the water made a broken second sky—a loon was swimming where her own young, a single one or two at most, must have been hidden.

The display of light in the north ended. And I went back inside the cabin, bare feet wet, chilled through in late July, and looked at my daughters asleep—the citizens of a vast country and of a vaster cosmos. But citizens of only a moment's time. Childhood, like the northern summer, is of such a sweetness that surely it was made to last. You would think that—would wish it, and sometimes almost believe it.

125

Then, in the fierce demonstration of brevities, the young are fledged, ice beards the reeds and, sudden as regret itself, the season turns.

57. *A Trick of Place and Time*

Memory is an unruly servant, like the butler in one of those dated English comedies. For years you imagine that he is in your employ, then one day you discover he has really become master of the house. You issue commands but they are ignored. The butler has a capricious will of his own.

One evening a fortnight ago, in a strange city, I observed a young couple out wheeling their infant in a carriage. They stopped at a bench in the little streetside park and took the baby from its buggy and sat holding and playing with their newborn while the life of the sidewalk flowed by. Hours later, back in my hotel room, there came over me the sudden realization that I could no longer remember the physical sensation of holding my own daughters as infants in my arms.

This discovery produced so keen a pang of sorrow that I actually gave a little cry aloud. That I *did* hold them—many times—I knew perfectly well. I even could call up a mental picture of the act, and some indistinct recollection of the pleasure it gave. But that was all an exercise of intellect. The true feeling of it, the exact *tactile sensation,* had been altogether lost.

Had those quiet moments been swept under and away by too much busyness? Was I simply inattentive? Or does it happen the same way to everyone? That I can't say. But as I look at my daughters now, plunging on toward young womanhood, most of their time in our care already elapsed, it is distressing to know that so rich an interval of one's life has fled beyond any power of deliberate recall. And yet, treacherous as memory is apt to be, it also is capable of wonders of quite the opposite sort.

Only a few days after that one I've mentioned, we were together in a boat, my daughters and I, here on this lake in the far north of Minnesota. As night came on, we determined to pursue a particular kind of fish. But where on all that water was it to be found, and how were we to know?

Darkness was deepening and far across the lake, from a bay behind a dark wooded point, the loons were sending up their cry of desolation. Nearly 50 years ago, when I was either 5 years old or 7, in the starry cold of just such a northern night I had crouched in the bottom of the boat on this very lake while my parents puzzled out and answered that same question about the fish. I had not thought about that in all the years since. But now, with memory as the navigator, I steered the boat to a place on the water that seemed as if it might be the right one.

With each oar stroke the picture in my mind came clearer. The risen moon was in the proper place. The curve of the reed bed was unquestionably the same. Suddenly, then, I was certain. The years rolled away with a rush, and my parents were there in the boat with us, as alive as they had ever been, their sharp cries of surprise ringing out over the water as they swung the many fish aboard.

In absolute faith we cast out our lines. And of course, the fish we sought—those and no others—were there.

Old as that memory was, it was as powerful and vivid as life itself. Which must mean that nothing really is ever lost, only oddly catalogued. Surely you have heard people of great age discuss this curiosity. The most distant events, they say, come readily to mind in exact detail. It is the recent ones that are clouded or mislaid entirely. They declare this a terrible vexation. But I count it to be a fine promise, at least where the matter of my daughters' early childhood is concerned.

The memory of them in my arms 15 years ago is irretrievable now. But with any luck I will survive long enough for that to become a matter of fairly ancient history. The girls will go out of our house. Their lives will take independent shape. They will have children in their time, if they choose to. And, if they do, the probability—the certainty you might almost say—is that those children will sometime be presented to me to hold.

And just as happened on the lake the other night under a certain slant of moon, all the clutter of years will pass from mind. In that instant, an old man will be very young once more. The life in his arms will be his own daughters as they were. And all that he imagined to be forgotten will be securely his again.

58. Riders on the Light

These northern days are uneven, undecided. One night will be chilly almost to the frosting point. Sharp-combed waves chop at the shore, and the sky spills a biting spit of rain. And you are certain you will wake to raw November. Then morning comes still and sunny, with a hum of fishermen's motors slicing the polished pewter of the lake toward the weed beds. Noon is warm as May again.

But everything alive is gripped now by a kind of end-of-season industry. Farmers are wrapping up and hauling their last cutting of hay. Wildflowers are glorious with the year's last bloom. Bands of deer, the bucks with antlers fully grown but still in velvet, advance in full daylight to the edge of the open meadow to browse and lay on fat against the ordeal ahead.

Ducks raft and rest in larger groups, already thinking south. The young ones of the late broods swim impatiently to and fro and try their wings, racing to learn the secret of the air while there is time. Yesterday, on a slough wrapped round by high marsh grass, we saw a beaver at work—gathering cuttings of young poplar to be chewed later in the months-long frozen darkness of his lodge.

And what are *we* storing up? A little memory of peace and ease, perhaps, to last the night through.

In early afternoons, when the sun is warmest, our daughters and the children of our friends splash at the lake's edge, then spread towels on the planks of the dock to absorb reflected light. They burn, but there is no future in it. Another month and they will be pale as the grubs found under forest logs.

Last night there was a meteor shower. The evening was absolutely clear and the vast showplace of the sky drew down closer than I ever can remember. We stood out on the grass, the children and I, shivering a little, and watched fragments of the universe fall toward us and incandesce, drawing sudden, brief lines of incredible brightness across the star map that glittered coldly at greater remove.

We looked outward through the band of suns as fine as dust, to the very rim of the Milky Way, strewn across the night with perfect clarity. We considered distances and time, the unreckonable meaning of a single light year, the barely imaginable events of suns cooling, dying—of *ours* dying, as it surely will—and the confusing way in which the messenger of light, on its journey across eternity, may deliver the news of events of primordial antiquity from places where there is only silent emptiness now.

What if we are only images carried on the light? they asked. *What is real, then? Where is the light of our time going? Who is watching to see it?* And other questions: *What is the universe? What greater thing is it a part of, and if the answer is that the universe is All, what is All, and what's beyond it? And how could any fraud peering at his earthly instruments pretend to know?*

Dizzy with inquiry, we stood with our faces tilted up, bound together by our common powerlessness before such mysteries. We felt ourselves shrinking, almost disappearing as we spoke. It was as if, in the next watch tick, we might be blown away to vanish among the stars.

Which is, of course, exactly how it happens. Though I didn't tell them that, and could not have made them believe—could not have explained how little our end-of-season industry counts for, ours or other creatures'. Or how, finally, that comes to seem unimportant, so long as there are other, younger images left to be carried on the light.

Amazed and a little lonely, then, we touched hands. And went inside.

III.

59. *Spacing the Losses*

A life is experienced most *painlessly,* if that's the word, when it is lived in unbroken continuity. Given a choice, I do not think I would much care to resume mine again after too long an interruption.

That odd thought occurred the other day when we returned from a few weeks away from the claims of the world, away from the press of obligations and the addictive stridency of the news, out of reach of all but the most urgent messages. Two weeks only. And what met us on return?

A note, first of all, written in sorrow by the young woman who was caring for them, that one of our cats had died. The oldest one—the woolly possumcat, the notched-eared stray who slept in her box beside the telephone, waiting for some call that never came. Never mind that we have a lot of cats. We have none to spare. And that one had been with us since the time of our children's first memories in another house.

After the note, the mail. Ordinarily I love to sort and open the mail. If I happen to be at home, I rush to snatch it from the box as soon as the postman's footfalls have receded down the drive. But out of the collected stack of it, the first letter, as it happened, bore bad news. In the second envelope was another and unrelated disappointment. So it went—the accumulation of ill tidings more than canceling out the half-dozen or so enticements to enter some sweepstake or other and become forever rich.

And there was more. Among our friends, a relationship had been overtaken and contorted by distress. A telephone call to the farm elicited word of several crises, none catastrophic but all demanding to be resolved. Our second car, the Asian instrument of my torment and financial ruin, when started up after sitting idle a while, gave out the unmistakable whinnies and *thunkings* of its imminent next collapse.

Now, the point is not that our despairs were any worse or more numerous than anyone else's. Of course they aren't. Occurring in the normal course of things, one or two a day over the span of weeks, they would have taken their place in the uneven pattern of events. The bad mixed with the good. Wounds, still, but with healing time between.

The trouble was in the concentration of them, received all at once.

I considered then, with greater understanding, all those people whose affairs have been interrupted in far worse and longer ways than by any vacation—by being held prisoners of war, or hostages of some terrorist gang, or by suffering any other involuntary absence of great duration. Naturally they yearn to come back to the world they knew. Their every thought is fixed on that.

But, in the actual moment of homegoing, how their eagerness must be qualified and confused by the dread of all they will find altered about that world. And the dread is well grounded. For the changes are sure to be many.

The current of events is irresistible, both the felicitous and the wretched. This mixture, lived day to day, can be easily enough endured and may even be described, on balance, as happiness. But the weight of it, thrust upon one collectively, may be insupportable.

At least, in a much smaller way, that was our experience.

It all has been dealt with. The farm needs have been met. The unpleasant letters have been answered. The old cat sleeps the last of summer through under a bush in the back yard, a little clutch of flowers marking the place. The children vow they'll take no more trips, ever. They cannot bear such hurts of coming back. Grief will soften, and that will change. But the experience has put them in touch with a somber truth, which is that the only people who are ever really safe are those with nothing and no one to leave, and therefore nothing much to come back to.

The rest of us have no sure defense.

60. *The Amazing Hunger*

Frustrated by a solitary run of days, with the women of the house away and no voices to be heard—days spent closed up in a bedroom with only the white cat, her dear but speechless friend, for company—the old dog has taken to eating things.

First she ate a telephone book. Next she ate a wastebasket and all its contents. Then part of a rug. Now she has started on a chair. She is reasonably continent and tidy, and gives no other reason for complaint. It is just that when I return from the office or from a few hours spent with friends I find some new part of the bedroom gone, disappeared inside her.

If her appetite were more limited, the veterinarian tells me—if she confined herself to eating dirt, say, or swallowing stones—the disease could be called *pica*. But her craving is comprehensive. And once begun, there seems to be no telling where it will end, for it is an addiction as relentlessly enslaving as alcohol or drugs or any that human beings suffer. And it is plain that she is powerless to stop herself.

A dog that has yielded to this behavior cannot be told superficially from any other dog. She does not waddle about with jaws agape, fangs clashing, swollen with all the strange stuff she has consumed. Her personality seems perfectly unchanged. She is docile and affectionate. It is only when she is left alone a while that depravity overcomes her. As you might imagine, this puts a certain suspense into the daily homecomings.

Climbing the stair and opening the bedroom door, I can tell right away if she has been on another binge. It's not necessary to look around the room, and anyway the eye may not immediately detect the absence of some object—a shelf of books, a piece of furniture—that has been swallowed up without a crumb. No, I can tell by her manner and her expression. Shame as profound as that is terrible to have to see in anything alive, whether it's a dog, a drunk or a dishonored politician.

She comes slinking slowly, guiltily, out from under the writing table. Her head hangs low in despair. She is a dog of considerable bulk, but in these moments she seems diminished in size by at least half. She rolls up her eyes to accept, to invite, the scolding she knows must come. They are old eyes, once deep chestnut brown but beginning to be dusted over by the blue of cataracts and full, now, of inexpressible regret.

Yes, I've been at it, she says, without saying anything. *I've given in to it again. I tried not to. After the last time I swore that I was finished—I'd never take another nip. But the day got long and no one spoke to me, no one touched me, and shadows came into the room. And, well, as you can see, or soon will, I've done something awful. I'm weak and contemptible. So what are we going to do about me?*

All that she is able to say with a look.

Nothing, I tell her. We're not going to do anything. A wastebasket never came to sit beside anyone and be stroked on a day when the world was full of loss and disappointment. No chair ever helped raise the children of the house. And rugs? Hell, rugs can be bought by the acre. We're not going to do anything. As long as there's a mattress in this bedroom left to lie down on—or even a well-chewed part of one—the bottom end of it is yours.

61. *Vacation Love*

The two girls are busy with secret projects in their rooms. One is preparing a package for the mail. The other has been at work on a letter, which, when some interruption causes her to lay it aside, she covers with another sheet.

I know the meaning of all this industry. And I know that when I am given these things to post, the addresses will say *Toronto*. It isn't that I've been spying. But I was young myself once, incredible as that must seem to them, and I remember vacation encounters. I remember a girl named Ruth, from the next cottage at a Minnesota lake. I eyed her reverently from a distance. And then somehow we met. We talked—not in the stiff, self-conscious way of being 14 years old, or whatever we were. We *really talked,* as human beings do, about things that mattered. Talk of the sort a vacation allows, between a boy and girl who probably will never see each other again—although, if prayers count and the universe is fair, they might.

She was, if I remember right, the first serious devotion of my life. I would have given her anything I owned. And if I hadn't, she could have claimed it by force. Because the silken goddess, Ruth, from the town of Mapleton not far away, was a robust Swede who towered above me by a minimum of a foot.

One day we swam on the pebbled beach below the cottages. Another day we rowed a small boat across the lake and sat talking for hours beside a clay bluff full of swallows' holes, and worried our families sick that we had drowned. She knew someone near there who kept horses. The last evening we had a picnic and went riding after dark with a lot of young people our same age. That was all. But it sufficed. It set that vacation apart from any before or for a long time after.

We wrote letters. And the universe *was* fair, in its way. I stopped through Mapleton to visit her several years later, when we both were nearly grown. She was engaged to be married, and showed me his picture. He was round-faced, with black hair slicked back against his head like an Italian tenor. I did not resent him. Nor did the years and her changed circumstance come between us. We talked as happily, as easily, as we had that long ago summer. I think it was because she had been for me the first girl—and I, perhaps, the first boy—ever to be known not as a strange and threatening member of the other gender, but as a friend.

For such a gift as that, one is grateful always.

The boys from Toronto I glimpsed several times, briefly, during our recent vacation. Twice at the tennis courts, another time at the beach. Besides English, they also spoke French with fluency, which gave them a fine sophistication. But of course the miracle at that age is to find a boy able to speak a civil or sensible syllable to girls in *any* language. For all I know, at home in Toronto they may be as mute and churlish as other lads. If so, vacation transformed them, as it once did me. So that, perfectly at ease, they and the girls spent hours engrossed in the novelty of conversation, trading information about themselves and their affairs.

That is what has provoked all this activity of wrapping packages and writing letters. Maybe, in the accident of things, they will meet again in that same place another year. It can be hoped. But either way they will surely remember—as I have, as who does not?—the first friendly step into a different, wider landscape of their lives.

62. *Waiting for the Birthday Suit*

"Surprise!" they cried, beaming like apes. "It's your birthday!"

"Surprise, nothing," I told them. "It's been my birthday on this same date every year for about 136 years. It is also the birthday of Amy Vanderbilt, Rose Kennedy, Pope Clement XI and Licia Albanese. Who cares?"

"Licia *Who*?" they said.

"You see what I mean? Who cares?"

"We'll get you a cake," they said. My daughters still foolishly imagine that birthdays, even mine and Licia Albanese's, are something to celebrate.

"Skip the cake," I told them. "It will go to my arterial walls like iron filings to a magnet. One bite of cake and I will turn a cyanotic shade of blue before your eyes." They seemed disappointed. "Just buy me an expensive present," I suggested, "and let it go at that. Something to memorialize my remaining potential as a wage-earner. Price is no object."

"Like what?" they said. "A red Porsche 911 Carrera?" They have become fluent in the nomenclature of foreign sports cars, for all the good it will ever do them. "There was one advertised last week. The

141

owner said he was willing to sacrifice it for not much more than you made last year."

"Then it's probably a junker," I said. "Been wrecked or something."

"Well, what else then?"

"You may have noticed that my station wagon is blowing purple smoke," I told them. "A valve job would be nice. Or a transmission overhaul. There might be some time when it would come in handy to have a reverse gear." Any mention of my station wagon always has a chilling effect on their automotive interest.

"We could get you a suit," they said. "Suits are expensive, aren't they?"

"About like cars," I said. "But I have a suit. Why would I want another one?"

"Because the one you have is lost."

"It *isn't either* lost. My suit is just having an adventure—wandering around the world on airplanes. The bag will be found. My suit will come home when it's ready."

"But it's been almost a month."

"What's a month?" I said. "A month is nothing. Like the greening and withering of one short season's grasses, a month is but a moment, an eye blink, in the life of any suit of mine. I'm not going to be in a hurry about that suit. The airline sure isn't."

It was plain that my attitude had demoralized them.

"You really know how to take the fun out of a birthday," they said.

"It's my day to spoil any way I want to."

"You're just a grouch in the morning. Tomorrow you'll feel different about it."

"You're right," I told them. "Tomorrow this will all be behind us." Just knowing that gives one the courage to carry on.

63. Failing Powers

So far, not many parts of me have had to be replaced. With the exception of my eyes, I am (if allowed moderate poetic license) pretty much the man I used to be. Only on such a morning as this one, when I have come away to the office leaving my glasses in the pocket of last night's coat, am I brought hard up against the facts of deterioration and the march of years.

My colleagues' faces blur and are unrecognizable. The walls and pillars of the newsroom where I work recede to distant grayness. This typewriter, my accomplice of many years, feels familiar to the touch— but I cannot be held accountable for what rises out of it. I have tried, in middle age, to cultivate a certain air of courtliness. Men's hands I shake. Women visitors I like to greet with a discreet kiss on the wrist or cheek. On a morning without my glasses I am more tentative, for fear the visitor might turn out not to be a lady at all, but the managing editor, and he would grow alarmed and possibly knock me down.

The problem with misplacing one's glasses is that, without them, one cannot see to find them. Often this happens while I am at home, or just preparing to leave.

"My glasses!" I cry out.

That single shouted announcement is enough. The entire family has been impressed with the importance of my glasses. Without them I cannot work. Meaning that there would be no food, no shoes, no allowances, no trips to anywhere. The children understand that the whole structure of their lives, in those moments, trembles on the edge of dissolution. The news is broadcast in shrieks of horror.

His glasses! Daddy's lost his glasses! Oh, sweet heaven, pray that we might find Daddy's glasses

143

before the people come to take the furniture and tow the car away!

There is a great rushing from room to room. I hear them passing through the ambient fog, groaning in their anxiety. Finally the glasses are found, or always have been. And are joyfully presented to me so that I may go serenely about doing whatever it was I had in mind—leaving my dependents queasy-stomached from their near miss.

Until now, my eyes are the only losable parts. But I am well aware that time's predations are cruel—that other functional elements of me will wear out in turn and have to be substituted for until, toward the end, I will be largely bionic. I have seen it happen. I remember my grandmother, late in life, observing wryly that she had become *only an appliance*. What's worse, this debilitation will coincide with my powerlessness in other matters.

For the moment, there is economic leverage. My wife and daughters have a keen interest in getting me to the office fit for work. But that will change. The girls will pass on through school to jobs and incomes of their own. There is no preventing it. My wife's business will flourish, or she will come into an unexpected inheritance. I will be pensioned off.

"My glasses!" I will cry out, then. And no one will seem to hear.

"My *teesh!*" I will demand petulantly. And the moist syllable will slide away to silence in that indifferent place.

64. *Loss Is the Lodger*

The house in which I am staying now, a guest, has emptied of its racket and confusion of several years ago. The sons have grown and gone. And the rooms from which one or another of them used to be displaced to make way for visitors are untenanted now.

Not empty, mind you. Just not regularly lived in anymore. The boys' rooms still are their own. Their books remain on the shelves—some of them, at any rate. Their saved articles from the various stages of boyhood still are to be seen on the walls and desks and on the fine old carved ledges above the doors. These leavings aren't preserved morbidly, as shrines. It is just that 20 years and more of occupancy make durable marks. If nothing else, nail holes in the wall must be kept covered. And what better way to cover them than to let hung things stay in their place?

So, if the boys ever were to come back here to live— back from Africa or the far West or the north country or the other side of town, wherever their luck has taken them—they would find the evidence of themselves remaining. In the natural way of growing up and growing away, however, that is unlikely to happen. Or, if it happens at all, not for long.

My friends, their parents, pretend to be untroubled by the stillness. Their own lives race forward, creative, occupied with ideas and values and the untiring defense of sense in a world tending ever toward senselessness. Or maybe they are not pretending. For with all their tenderness they are realists. They grew up and went away themselves. They know it happens. Even so, I have to think that sometimes, in the quiet of the evening, they must look up from a book or the stack of papers to be graded and listen for a footstep on the stair. Or, in passing the open door of one of these upstairs rooms, that they might, just for an unguarded instant, find it odd to see the bed unslept in.

They don't speak about that, though. Humanity's a game of losses. And grace is learning to take yours with a poker face. With other creatures it's different. With a cat, for instance.

Today, with a bit of writing to do, I turned on the lamp in one of the unoccupied upper rooms and arranged myself and my working things at the borrowed desk. Above the door at the left were two footballs. On the bookcase behind, a model ship. On the table at the right, some arcane mechanical construction and also an empty bottle of Irish beer. On the desk's top was a wind-up alarm clock with its spring run down. And in the desk drawers were— among other things—a box of broken crayons, a fuzzless tennis ball, assorted small bicycle parts and a folder marked *"Personal Letters,"* into which I had the decency not to pry.

Having oriented myself by these investigations, I began to work. But before very long I sensed a presence near at hand. It was the cat of the house, sitting in the doorway, sizing up the situation with cool green eyes.

The meaning of what followed could not have been plainer if the cat had suddenly been empowered to speak her thoughts aloud. By her puzzled expression, it was obvious the look of me sitting there at the desk was somehow slightly wrong. And possibly the smell of me as well. Yet, at the same time, she found it good to see the room again in use—the lamp burning, the chair sat it, papers scattered and one of those man animals busy with his incomprehensible occupations.

So she rose, the cat did, and came a bit uncertainly across the threshold. I put down my hand and she examined it and slightly shied away. It was not the proper hand. But then she relented and let herself be stroked. The foot and leg, too, were somehow wrong.

146

She turned those green eyes up directly into my own with a speculative look.

Who the hell are you? she demanded to know. *You're not the one who used to sit there—who ought to be sitting there again.* But then she appeared to have an afterthought. Better an old boy than no boy at all, her manner seemed to say. Anyway, a room needs to be lived in. The lamp shone warmly. The clutter of papers and the click of the typewriter were reassuring. So she flung herself against my trouser leg, and rubbed there companionably. And then, quite satisfied, demanded to be let outside to explore the autumn yard.

I will be sorry for her sake—for her sake only—to gather up my things one day shortly and leave the room to silence and to her memories again. Cats do not know how to conceal their losses. Cats, contrary to their reputation, can't lock their hurts behind a poker face. If you imagine otherwise you don't know cats. Or losses.

65. I Can't Manage the Universe

The planet tilts a fraction in its spinning, and suddenly the midday brilliance of our star is bearable, the nights are fresh for sleeping and the hour of getting up is blue again.

Yesterday, some creature began a hole alongside our house foundation, throwing up a tailing of mealy dirt at the entrance of its burrow. Today, I saw the proprietor of that hole dart across the driveway and vanish in a patch of undergrowth. A chipmunk was who he was—autumn fat, but caught up in the season's fury of preparation.

I meant to fill his excavation—scoop the earth back in, tamp it firm and maybe put a rock atop the place for good measure. He might have a house to make, but I have one to guard. I actually went so far as to fetch the shovel. But then I measured the product of all that digging against the size of the digger, and found that, in the end, I couldn't do it. Next spring, maybe, but not now, not in the year's changing. The porous basement wall won't be fatally hurt by one more seep. Not the way that things alive can be hurt by bad luck or error in this season.

Managing the universe would be an awful responsibility to have to bear—deciding which things would bite and which be bitten, which ones would spin webs and which be caught in them, which ones would sleep a winter safely through and which perish with the frost. Complicated judgments, those, and very final. And the accident of belonging to the race of things that hammers iron and makes shovels may not entitle one to meddle in the process.

That was my line of reasoning, anyway, about the chipmunk and his hole. From his perspective I may loom fairly omnipotent. But I know better. Like him, I'm just another creature bearing on toward the solstice, with only so much margin for error, only so much credit to spend. And from this recognition flows a certain passivity, a flabbiness of will that worsens year by year.

As in the matter of the kitten that, a fortnight ago, presented itself a slight and large-eyed wanderer at our door. Yes, *another* one. Harden your hearts, I commanded, but my daughter let it in. All right, then, we'll *give it away*. Then the heat of summer broke. A cool wind sent leaves spinning down. The cat, never once imagining the world might have no place for it, found the food dish, the softest chair cushion, the place on the window sill where the late sun falls. Made homage to the older cats and was accepted. Reached a friendly understanding with the dogs. And finally, in the dark of one morning, like the others before it, was discovered beside us in the bed.

He's one of us now. Tardily, some folks have said they'd like to have him. But nothing could persuade us to give him up. He's a cat beyond price. Just as that chipmunk is my chipmunk, and I'll have no stranger or neighbor messing with his hole.

Daughters and mothers . . . wives and hunting dogs . . . dogs and cats . . . cats and chipmunks . . . chipmunks and deed-holders of wet foundations— where, in any of that, is there an easy fit? Into the dark of the year we go together, and I take no responsibility. Whatever flung us together will have to sort us out.

66. *Perishable Celebrity*

We love most intensely that creature or that thing which we fear may soon be lost to us. The thing itself has not changed at all. But the imminence of its loss has made it priceless. Consider the example of snail darters and pupfish and the whooping crane.

Probably not one person in a thousand—or in 100,000—had heard of the snail darter until a few years ago. Whole generations had gone to their graves without ever speaking its name, and so might ours have. Except that the damming of a certain river was proposed. The snail darter was found to live in that river and, worse yet, was determined to be rare. And as with all the other creatures we have driven to survival's edge, that small fish became the instant object of fierce and quite widespread devotion.

Now the snail darter has entered into the popular vocabulary and become a part of our national consciousness. As the minnow goes, so goes public morality. If the snail darter perishes, ring down the long twilight of ruin. In the same way, I have known people to drive several hundred miles round-trip on the chance—an outside chance at that—of seeing a whooping crane in the wild. And an authenticated report of a particular variety of pupfish observed gasping in some fetid desert puddle has been known to cause ecstasy of the sort usually inspired by the rose window in the Cathedral of Chartres.

Beauty is not the point. Probably the same passion would develop for cockroaches and dung beetles if there were known to be only seven of them left alive on Earth. But love is fickle. Let it be discovered that the snail darter is not endangered after all, that in fact there are whole river systems in which he teems in inestimable numbers, and our ardor for him will quickly cool. Let the whooping crane multiply beyond a certain point and you will hear him mentioned, if at all, only in terms of the fitness of his meat for table.

All this is prologue.

A cat of ours became ill not long ago. The ailment wasn't serious but we did not know that at the time. The symptoms were ominous. Now, this particular cat had a bad habit or two. Never mind just what those were—suffice that they were bad. But with the onset of the illness, it was amazing how these faults of his were brushed aside by our sudden new appreciation of his general excellence.

He became, for several days, the central figure in our household. He was endlessly held and comforted and stroked. His name was being spoken constantly and his virtues recited. He could do no wrong. There even was talk of letting him outdoors. Because of the hazard of dogs and street, he had been until then mostly an inside cat. But he crouched at the crack of the door with an awful longing, and now guilt assailed us. What was the use of confining him? What were we protecting him from—except life itself? And if his days were short, what use, what mercy, was caution now?

In due course he was examined. The results were inconclusive, and our concern mounted. He was taken to another city for tests of a more elaborate and more expensive sort. By this time cost did not matter, so great was his surpassing fineness as a cat. Then the news was received, along with the bill.

The news was that he was not sick at all. Never had been. The symptom that so alarmed us had been just one of those things that happens from time to time with cats—a minor indisposition that has, and needs, no explanation. You would not believe the change of attitudes. He must wonder again why his name is so rarely spoken, except when linked with a curse at his old habits. If he mews at the crack of the door, a shoe toe moves him brusquely, and pitilessly, aside. He is just a cat again. A cat that cost a lot.

His symptoms have disappeared entirely. Gone, too, is any memory of the lesson we might have learned. We have become indifferent and unforgiving once more. That's how it goes with snail darters and cats and all the other things and creatures in our lives— even the people in them—when we imagine they will last forever.

67. *Raking It In*

Now that their desire for cash has grown beyond my ability to supply it, my daughters' view of the world is colored by need. And the result is not all bad.

Take leaves, for example. A leaf on the branch has always struck me as a thing of beauty, providing shade, exhaling oxygen, feeding the caterpillars that will become next year's butterflies, no doubt performing other useful services. The leaves of autumn can set a whole street alight with color.

But eventually they make their final pilgrimage from branch to ground, and become a monstrous clutter—crisping, rotting, hiding the thrown newspaper, turning the sidewalk slimy with every rain. I used to own a leaf rake. Then one year the man in the next house east lent me his. I broke it, and after while he came and took the pieces back. So while I am perfectly aware that my yard each October is an offense to order along the block, I am without the technology to set it right. That's not an excuse. It's a fact.

How pleasant it was to learn, the other day, that what I have considered an oppressive nuisance my daughters regard as a valuable natural resource, a crop. "I need to earn some money," one of them said. "Can I rake the leaves?"

"Why not?" I told her. "Probably the leaves ought to be raked every four or five years, whether they need it or not."

"How much can I make?"

I seemed to remember that it was about a 35- or 40-bag yard. "You'll make a lot," I told her. "Ten dollars at a minimum."

"You're kidding! A measly 10?" Her eyes were hard, like a Teamsters negotiator dealing with the owner of a 50-truck fleet of refrigerated fish.

"Ten for you," I said quickly, "and 10 for your sister."

"Don't tell *her*. It's my job. Where's the rake?"

"There isn't any rake," I told her. "I'm not going to make a major investment in this. Anyway, there's no use starting until all the leaves are down. You can see, a lot of them still are up there."

She sized up the trees.

"When will the rest fall?"

"Any day now. The first good wind or driving rain."

"But some of them still are green."

"That will give you time to earn some money to buy a rake."

"You're cheap," she said.

"Welcome to the world of commerce," I told her. "You're not a kid anymore. If you don't want the work I will bid the job out to your sister."

"And you're mean."

"I'm just a businessman. It's supply and demand, and I've got the leaves."

"What if the people from the neighborhood association come around again?"

"I'll tell them I'm having labor problems."

"They never believe you."

"That's all right. Pretty soon it will snow and the leaves will be covered up."

"When it snows," she said, "can I shovel the walk?"

"Of course," I told her. "If you buy a shovel."

"But how do I get money for a shovel?"

"Rake the leaves."

Keep them barefoot and poor long enough and, somehow, the work gets done.

68. *The Years Before the Chair*

The bird dog, Rufus, gets worthless and a little crazy in the idle months, but he has begun again to sober and steady. It always happens when the days shorten and the nights cool.

I don't know how much, if anything, he understands of time. But the changing light and the different smell of paling grass are signs he can read perfectly. In the withering-down and drying of the season, the message carried to him on the air has begun to resolve itself into a sense of something he remembers well.

Stone-still inside the wire of his run, he fixes his cool yellow stare on the birds that trespass through the air space of the yard. He knows their name: *Bird.* After his own name, it was the first word in his slim vocabulary. He also knows they are not exactly the right ones of their kind. But they are alike enough to be suggestive. He waits until they pass from view, then watches for the next ones.

From earliest puppyhood he's had those strange eyes. Soft-natured and playful, he is, a tail-wagging terror-slave of the cats. Yet sometimes when he turns his gaze on you there is the fleeting, odd sensation that his eyes are not windows, as the old dog's are. The color, exactly, of pale Baltic amber, they see all but give nothing back. It is like looking at a one-way glass.

This autumn will be his fourth—the fourth of the eight or 10 good ones he'll have. After that, with luck, it will be just the house, the rug, the soft bedroom chair. He loves that chair now with a passion that is almost indecent. But when those later autumns come and his legs won't carry him as fast or far, he'll learn to love it less.

It's another busy year. The calendar gets cluttered. There isn't, reasonably, time enough for truant days spent wandering across field, fording creeks, shouldering through underbrush. Too much of that can chill a marriage, cripple a career. One has to have priorities. On the other hand . . .

It's not just a wife and a boss a man has to live with. He also has to live with himself. A long time ago I had two beagle friends. We must have spent a couple of hundred days afield together. Then life changed. I got distracted by other things for what seemed a minute, and when I looked again they were white-muzzled and sore of leg. After they were gone, it wasn't the rabbits they'd run that I remembered. It was all the ones they *hadn't* run because the man who kept them fenced,

154

though he cared for them a lot, had bigger fish to fry. That's more guilt than anyone ought to have to carry.

Responsibility is a fine word, but lifeless. The calendar's a nag. A wife is understanding, and a boss is forgiving, or had better be. Rufus has a gift, a calling. It would be pure selfishness, I tell myself, to put my work ahead of his. He goes now, at evening, to his place on the upholstery. He whines a little in his sleep, and his feet twitch as he runs through some birdy dream. He may suspect a certain splendid morning is near. He can't know that morning is tomorrow.

The years will go like leaf smoke, and with them any record of our misbehavior. We'll have a long time, he and I, to remember the best of autumn and learn to hate the chair.

69. *A Science Career on Ice*

You have known people who sifted endlessly, wistfully, through the cold ashes of circumstance in hope of explaining the odd turns their lives took. *If only a certain train had not been late . . . If only I'd gone to Toledo instead of Louisville on that day . . . If only Henry, not Albert, had taken me for that ride on his motor scooter . . . Everything afterward might have been different.*

Someday, stumbling along the alleys of an uncaring city, her dreams a ruin and everything she owns in a plastic bag, my daughter may wonder how her chance was lost. The plans for higher education, a useful career, the reward of accomplishment—gone, all of it. Snatched from her, in the very flowering of her

155

C. W. Gusewelle

promise, by a single night's untimely frost. And the resulting scarcity of bugs.

She does not remember, precisely, when the science assignment was announced, but it was some weeks ago. In the sweet languor of summer ending and autumn just beginning, there are better things to do than go grubbing through the unwholesome jungle of the yard, collecting things that creep on too many legs and squirt nasty juices and maybe bite. Later. It can be done later. Bugs, after all, are everywhere.

Sit outside at evening with a glass in hand, and clouds of them come boiling out of the undergrowth to feed on exposed flesh. Serve refreshments to guests on the patio, and in the light of the citronella candles bugs can be seen crawling over the *hors d'oeuvres* and clinging like fat kernels of caramel popcorn to the smart dresses of the ladies. Bugs bat ceaselessly against the outer screens. In the gloom of the basement, sly squads of them circulate restlessly from dark of crevice to secret damp of drain. The dogs and cats are dusted regularly with poison powder. A day later, they are again nipping at their underparts and peering into their own fur, alert to any small, quick movement.

So anything as unnatural as a lack of bugs has never occurred to us. Then, in a night of record chill, the window of opportunity slammed shut.

Fifteen insects, she is required to have. Skewered with pins and mounted in some orderly way, all identified. If she doesn't get them, I assume her schooling stops here and we'd just as well send her off directly to gasp away what's left of girlhood, inhaling cotton fibers and changing the spindles in some Georgia textile mill.

Except for the frost, it would have been easy. But now, with bugs vanished and with so much riding on it, the resources of the whole family have been flung into the project. My wife has received from a friend the firm promise of a cockroach. Left unpowdered for a

156

week, the cats should be productive—if somehow it is possible to get a pin through a flea without spoiling the specimen. There are moths in the coat closet, and a wasp nest under the roof eave. I have gotten off a letter to an old army buddy, asking if he might chip in a crablouse.

So we are more or less at five, and counting. Fifteen seems out of reach. In desperation, I have put out a plea in the newspaper column I write, asking any readers who happen to find something moving in their hair or clothing if they would be so kind as to drop it by my office in an envelope or small jar. I wouldn't ask that for myself. It's for my daughter, whose tomorrows have all but slipped away.

70. *The Gift of Plenty*

The festive spirit has claimed our house. The floors are polished. The rugs and upholstery have been cleansed of the malfeasances of dogs and cats. Friends will be joining us at tomorrow's table, and I must rise in the darkness of early morning to stuff and bake the Thanksgiving opossum.

Probably there will be snide comments. Our friends are not the kind of people who hide their contempt under a bushel.

"What's that thing on the platter?"

"It's the Thanksgiving possum," I will reply evenly, as I carve. "Light meat or dark?"

A mutter of outrage will pass among them.

"Is this some kind of joke? We're supposed to get turkey. It's a national tradition."

"Since when?"

"Since the Pilgrims. The Indians brought the Pilgrims a turkey."

"Listen," I will tell them, "the Pilgrims were a bunch of losers, down on their luck. Winter was coming on and they were hungry. Then the Indians showed up with some food."

"With a turkey."

"Okay, so it was a turkey. But it could have been anything. Some days the Indians had buffalo tongue. Other times it was porcupine or bear meat. That day they they just happened to have a turkey. *Big deal!*"

"Are you implying that Turkey Day is an empty tradition?"

"I am only saying that if the Indians had come with a possum, the Pilgrims—who were a sorry, rag-tag outfit—would have been mighty glad to get it. They would have smacked their lips and declared that henceforth, forever, the last Thursday in November would be known as Possum Day. People would stand in line at the supermarket to get their Butterball possums."

"You got that thing at a store?"

"No, it was a gift."

"From an Indian?"

"A gift of luck. I got it yesterday afternoon on Bannister Road with my right front tire, a glancing blow. It was hardly even bruised."

The guests will sit with their clenched fists on the table beside their plates, knives and forks sticking straight up from their fists. They will make no effort to hide their disappointment.

"The last time we came for Thanksgiving you had a turkey."

"That was the last time. Before they went off half-cocked to the New World to starve as Pilgrims, the Pilgrims sat around their cozy fireplaces in London and ate plum pudding. Things change. Now I am a man in the twilight of his powers, with two daughters still to put through college, and I am a rag-tag Pilgrim who takes what he is given. If a turkey had crossed the road yesterday, we would have had turkey. What I was given, however, was a possum. We will eat it together in fellowship and gratitude."

"Not me!"

"Me either!"

The drumming of the handles of their knives and forks on the table will make an awful racket.

"For the blessings of this day," my daughters will intone reverently. "And for the blessings of financial aid and federal student loans that may yet be received . . ."

Shamed to silence, our guests will stare at the main course.

"Here we are, all together once more!" I will sing out heartily. "The harvest is in. The frost is on the punkin and the corn is in the shock."

They will look back at me with gray, flat faces.

"So speak up now," I will tell them again, "light meat or dark?"

71. A Night Call

The largest troubles come with an awful suddenness. Almost never is anyone forewarned. For days and years uninterrupted, lives proceed stolidly on their accustomed march. Then, in an instant, all is at terrible risk.

A friend telephoned last night. The call came late in the evening—at an hour when most of us, by cruel experience, have learned to fear the instrument's ring. The friend had news to tell. She spoke it haltingly, in a voice made strange and thin by her fear.

Their family, she said, had passed two nightmare weeks. The younger of the two sons of the household had received a physical examination for high school athletics and of course had been pronounced perfectly fit. Only days later, however, he had sickened. And had undergone major surgery for a cancer which threatened his life. That quickly had they all been flung into torment and their lives disarranged.

The boy was out of the hospital, she said—had come home yesterday. She told what she had prepared for dinner, and that he had been able to eat. In the weeks ahead he will return for a course of therapy with powerful chemicals. But between those treatments, which are expected to be punishing, he will live and study at home.

It has not been very long since we stopped with those friends during an end-of-summer trip to the Colorado mountains. Theirs is a lovely home, located just where a sweep of grass and boulders mounts up to the base of the foothills, with the greater peaks beyond. We passed two days and nights there, and spoke of the happy rhythm of their lives in that place. They are old friends, so we have watched their children grow. The oldest is away at college. The youngest is our own daughters' age.

The middle one, the younger boy, is both an athlete and a gifted artist. We remarked how handsome he had grown to be, and how much taller, in the two years since last we'd seen him.

"The doctors say the operation was successful," his mother said on the phone last night. "And it's a kind of cancer that's curable. We're holding on to that." She pronounced the words as if in a dream, though, and could not keep her voice from trembling with fright. We replied with testimony of concern and affection. And also of encouragement, for whatever belief that might command. She hung up, then—in her home a long day to the west, in that fine place just under the brow of the mountain. And we sat for several moments unspeaking, still feeling the alarm of the call at that hour.

Earlier in the day, some worry or other had been dogging us. Abruptly it was gone from mind, pushed aside and made inconsequential by our friend's distressing news. Rarely does one have a set of troubles that cannot be made to seem small alongside someone else's.

The boy is young and strong and otherwise wonderfully healthy, we said finally, to one another. *And surely that will work in his favor. Surely the nightmare will somehow end well.* This conversation was interrupted by a cry from down the hall, from the room where our daughters had been working late on school assignments. They were demanding that we come to see them off to sleep with proper ceremony.

The ritual of tucking them in their beds used to be invariable. But years have passed and the girls have grown almost past being children any more. And bedtime has become a less formal, a more perfunctory event. Sometimes we are away. Or they are. Sometimes we have been emptied out by the claims of the day— too tired for rituals, too impatient just for silence in the house. Sometimes we are caught up in a task that we imagine cannot be interrupted. Or some vexation or disappointment—small, but seeming large—has rooted us despondent in a chair.

For whatever reason, we sometimes haven't the spirit for it. Or the time.

How long we will be affected by the memory of our friend's telephone call I can't say. We hope, of course, when next we hear from her, that the news will all be good and her voice will be free of fear again. Last night, when just after speaking to her we were summoned by our daughters—wanting only a few quiet, uninterrupted minutes of ourselves—how quickly, how gladly, we went to them. Believe me, there was time.

72. *Memory of the Wolf*

Usually the wail of a far-off siren begins it.

The yellow dog across the street replies with a howl. Then that one is joined by another from the yard behind. Then others add their voices from a distance. And finally even the bird dog, Rufus, not given much to speaking, points his muzzle skyward and sings his part.

I used to wonder why they did it. It couldn't be out of loneliness, because all those are house dogs—each one secure in his pack, whose members are the people and other creatures of the house. It occurred that maybe they imagined the siren was some great dog god, who, when he called to them from a distance, had to be answered.

But it's nothing as mystical as that, the books say. It's something quite explainable, though in its way, when you think about it, maybe even more fabulous. The siren speaks, and across an unremembered eternity of more than 30 million years, maybe nearer 40 million, the *wolf* in all of them replies.

He is the oldest of man's creature friends, the dog. His bones have been found beside the cold ashes of 10,000-year-old hearths. His shape has changed in uncountable ways, from hairless terrier that can be held in the palm of one hand to something almost as great and shaggy as a bear, and all the possibilities between. He has learned to work—to fetch, find game, herd our other creatures, smell out drugs and felons, guard our property, guide us through the sightless dark, do circus tricks. Animal psychologists say he even can understand a bit of our language, 40 words of it or, if he's precocious, perhaps as many as 60.

In return for the comfort of kennel or rug, he has traded away a good many of his skills, become a hostage to food bowl and grub that comes canned or sacked. He's a kept thing that wears a collar, goes walking on a leash. Abjectly he rolls over to present his stomach for scratching.

Then he hears the siren's howl, telling the news of a kill somewhere out there in the vastness of a wild savannah. And whatever shape he happens to have taken, whatever obliging habits he has learned, the ancient wildness in him hears the message and calls a reply. Think of that, when you look in the eyes of the dog of your house. I do, when I trade a stare with Rufus or Cinnamon, the portly matron half-hound who trembles at the drumroll of every thunderstorm.

I think I know you, I tell the dog. *But how can I ever really know that part of you that is so incredibly old?* The dog looks blankly back, most of those not being among the 40 known words. And almost in that same moment, I think of myself and of my own kind.

How much old baggage do we carry? I am wondering. *What memories of blood and fire, of clanship and violence, of terror and brutal rage? And if the siren howls again for us, how long do we keep ourselves from answering?* And I am a little frightened, then, not by the wolf in the dog but by something like the wolf inside us all.

73. *The Careful, Lonely Heart*

She would forgive me, I think, for speaking of this. It was not really a confidence shared, just a small aside in a letter to a stranger about another matter.

163

Her mother, she wrote, recently had died. The mother had lived with her and she expected that the loss she now felt—the void, as she described it—would be hard to fill. She had thought of getting a pup, she said. Then she followed that with a plaintive phrase: *"But since I am nearing 50, I may be inviting more heartbreak."* The letter turned back to business then. And was duly put out of mind . . . except for that one comment and the curious note of dread that it contained.

Several days later I found myself still wondering: Where would anyone possibly find a danger of heartbreak in a pup? But after a little consideration I thought I understood what she meant. It was not the creature itself that would bring hurt. The danger lay in the affection she would surely come to feel for it, thus exposing her to the risk of yet another loss.

Is there anyone who has not, some time or other, shared a little of that same despairing caution? The losses of a life accumulate. Some people's are greater, others' may be less. But they come to us all. There are times when the collection of them seems all but insupportable, and when the addition of just one more—never mind its precise dimension—might cause the bearer to sink away forever under that baggage of griefs.

We defend ourselves against the imminent collapse by a variety of means, not all of them healthy or even reasonable. Children who very early have sustained a great loss may be reluctant afterward to form deep attachments. For some, this tragic incapacity is lasting and incurable.

Age, then, has nothing to do with it. The writer of that letter said she was nearing 50. Well, I am well past that mark. And when I inventory the several cats and dogs of our household—each with its own character, each greatly loved—I am reminded often that some way, some time, we will lose them all. I hate the prospect. If there were any breed that came guaranteed to last for the duration, I would keep no other kind, regardless of its shape, color or expensive appetites. But there is no such animal.

So when the pain arrives, as surely it will, our answer to it—the only useful one I know—will be immediately to reinvest ourselves in other creatures. And after those, still others. Because the alternative is terrible to imagine.

I knew a dog once that had spent his entire puppyhood in a fenced run, with food and water shoved under the wire and the cement floor hosed out occasionally. In all that time, three or four years, he did not once feel the touch of a caring hand. When, at last, he was taken from the cage, that dog was a pitiable case.

The loss he had suffered—the loss not just of affection but of contact of any appreciable sort—had warped him beyond remedy. When people sought to make a pet of him he fled, cowered under outbuildings, trembled so that his teeth could be heard clattering, refused to be touched. He may sometimes briefly have wondered (if speculation is possible for a dog) whether, by the remotest of chances, those people meant kindness. But it was inconceivable that a world as indifferent as the one he had known could intend anything but abuse.

At any rate, he never took the risk. He was tamed, after a fashion. But 10 years later, even in the last year of his life, when you stroked him you could feel him trembling under your hand, still waiting for the expected blow.

That is the ultimate consequence of taking no chances of the heart.

74.   The Long Shadow

The dog grows older and fatter and has developed a taste for roast duck in sherry sauce. Our pets are mirrors of ourselves.

The house begins to show the wear of time. Cold drafts whine at the door corners. The basement is a jungle of things saved and things forgotten. Our dwellings personify our natures and the patterns of our lives.

The children advance in years. Their talents begin to be manifest. One imagines the future at their command, but it is only partly so. All the past is in them, too. Our children replicate most of our mistakes. We cast long shadows.

My father's unhandiness with tools, his defeat in the face of the smallest task of domestic repair, have become mine in turn. But so, I think, has something of his credulous faith in the goodness of the people he met. From my mother has come a fondness for the out-of-doors and silent places, a certain romanticism and an ear for melancholy.

My wife's father had a gift for gardening and for working with wood. Thus, when I see her with trowel in hand or rubbing stain into an old piece of furniture to restore its luster, I see him very much alive in her. Her mother was a wonderfully humorous and idiosyncratic lady. She loved words and, in her speech, combined them in phrases and usages peculiarly her own—at once so utterly odd and so perfect that they lodged forever in the mind. My wife speaks those phrases still. And, just the other day, I heard one of them spring unbidden to the lips of my youngest daughter. For all time, for as many generations as our line endures, they will continue to be spoken and heard.

Examine carefully enough any of the components of one's attitudes and behavior—the values one holds, the habits one obeys—and the origin nearly always can be discovered.

Belief in the transcendent power of ideas I can trace back to a particular professor to whom I had the luck to be exposed in the 18th through the 21st years of my life. My sense of the journalist's craft has come mainly from the newspaper folk for whom, and with whom, I have been privileged to work. From a friend I stood beside in frozen duck marshes at an impressionable age there came an intemperate passion for winter dawns and sunsets and the whisper of quick wings in the darkness. From my wife, an addiction to the majesty of mountains.

And so it goes. We are born understanding nothing, caring about nothing. Everything, or nearly everything, is borrowed. Tennyson spoke of that, although more eloquently, as you'd expect. In the poem, "Ulysses," the aged wanderer looks back across a life of far adventure and says: *"I am a part of all that I have met."*

As we all are—all of us borrowers. The sum of our borrowings becomes the creature called ourselves, and presently we are borrowed from in turn. Nameless and unattributed, these oddities and small glories pass then into the collective experience of our kind. That is the longest shadow we cast. There is no particular fame in it, and it is far from what some people have in mind who speak of immortality. But, for most of us, it may have to do.

75. Tolerating Trespass

Incursions upon our territory by creatures in any way unlike ourselves can inspire strange and terrible behavior. There is no disputing that.

Once in a great while—years between—one reads of the appearance of a bear in some settled section of a countryside where no bears were thought to be. Never mind that these bears almost always are of the smallish and retiring variety. Or that, lost, frightened, obliged to rummage in dumps and garbage cans, the bear would like nothing more than to be returned to the forest from which it has strayed. Or that the law in such cases usually prescribes entrapment, not destruction.

Always the response is the same. Men and boys of that neighborhood take to field and wood like a savage army, armed with everything from heavy rifles to hay forks, and range yowling over the countryside until the offending beast finally is brought to bay and slain. Sometimes the hunters shoot and wound each other. But from the first report until the army limps home in triumph, the end is known. *The bear must be killed.*

The intruder need not even be that large. Once I had gone to a man's shop to visit with him about a business matter. And in the course of our talking the subject of mice somehow came up. It had been a bitter winter, and more than the ordinary number of mice, he said, had found their way indoors.

No sooner had he mentioned this than a mouse showed itself—a fawn-colored little mouse, making its way timidly across the cement shop floor. Its eyes were dull and it seemed to move sluggishly, perhaps sickened by poison that had been set out. The man gave a shout of outrage and leaped forward, bringing his foot down on the mouse to end its trespass. Now,

I know him to be a decent man, capable in his business, good to his family. But after that, whenever we have met, I have remembered that ghastly moment in his shop. I cannot forget the sound his shoe made when he brought it down—or what was left on the pavement when he lifted it again matter-of-factly to inspect his work.

These thoughts were brought to mind, in the context of greater violence in the world, when, a quarter of an hour or so ago, I noticed a spider crawling across my desk.

Spiders are the enemy. Their purposes and their ideology, if they have one, are different from ours. Not even the charming story of Charlotte, the spider who wove wondrous messages in her web, has succeeded in anthropomorphizing and making them likable. Quite a small spider, this one was, no more than an eighth of an inch across, bound on some errand that led from the calendar pad, where I first detected it, across a stack of papers toward a crevice where the desk comes up against a filing cabinet.

This desk is mine. I occupy it most days, and earn my living seated at it. Whether that qualifies the desk as my sacred territory I can't say. I only knew I didn't want the spider creeping where he was. So I raised a folded magazine and took aim—*locked on the target,* so to speak. I was prepared, in the cold euphemism of power, to terminate the creature's incursion. The hand that held the magazine needed only a command from the brain.

But the command did not come. What came instead was a sense of the absurd discrepancy between my size and that of the spider. And also memories of those accounts of men yammering in pursuit of bears, and of that mouse exploded under a shoe.

Unfolding the magazine, then, I put it back with the others on the stack. And watched the tiny spider complete its march and disappear into the crevice behind the cabinet, there no doubt to multiply its kind and perhaps even to plan further and more impudent challenges to my desktop sovereignty. An accident had saved him—the accident of things remembered, and worse things lately in the news. Maybe I will regret it. But I cannot help feeling that the claim to civilization is bought at certain risk.

76. *The Humble Mourner*

"I'm afraid we're losing him," she said. And I told her, "No, he'll be all right, believe me." Because I wanted more than anything for that to be true.

She was right, though, and I was wrong. The veterinarian called, and in a gentle voice—because the veterinarian also is a friend—he said, "I was holding him at the end. There's nothing else we could have done." And in those few words, the great white cat, Oliver, passed from our lives, taking a bit of all of us with him.

I don't mean to make too much of this. Life is composed in the half part, at least, of losses. And we have friends whose losses have been so terrible as not even to be decently mentioned in the same breath as this one of ours.

What's more, in remembering him, there's no use idealizing. He had his faults—was vain and pugnacious in his younger years, grew misanthropic and demanding as he aged. But he also could be wonderfully tender when it suited him. And toward the last, it suited him more and more.

He had a way of insinuating himself under an arm or onto the pillow beside your head as you slept. He had fine, intelligent eyes and a large, regal head, like a statue lion. He looked directly at you when he spoke, and, with patience, he taught us a few of his words.

He arrived when the children were small, and lasted until they are now about to leave. Oliver and the old dog were young together. They slept pressed side by side, and washed each other's ears. Then more cats came, and after those a rowdy pup, and always he accommodated. Each time he was the one who offered peace. It's what you can do, if you're confident of your place.

We discussed it briefly. I'm not much for burying in a wet yard in the cold of winter, So he's gone to ashes, and when the ground unfreezes we'll put those beside a tree he liked to scratch, and in the spring we'll plant a flower there.

Before he was committed to the fire, I went to the veterinarian's place for a last visit in the privacy of one of the small examining rooms. He was so little changed. I took his ear between my fingers and felt the familiar little bump that was a healed scar of antique battle. I touched his whiskers that, brushing at my face, so often tickled me awake. His fur was soft under my hand.

It helped to do that, though I'm glad there was no one there to watch.

That evening we talked, and shared our pain in remembering. We toasted, with raised glasses, the wonder of a cat he'd been. And it seemed we might muddle on more or less all right from there. But in a small hour of night, the door opened and the brightness from the hall fell suddenly on our bed. It was one of our daughters, standing there against the light.

"The old dog," she said, her voice broken. *"She's going from room to room.* She can hardly see, but she's trying to find him." In our selfish sadness, we'd forgotten about the dog.

We listened, then. And we could hear: Pacing tirelessly from one corner of the house to the other, her nails clicking on the wood of the floors below, understanding nothing, perhaps sensing everything, half-blinded by cataracts but hunting, hunting with her nose for the nearness of her friend, the cat of all her years.

Grief is grief. Even in its humbler forms it's sometimes damned near insupportable.

77. A Holiday Dream

The season again came catapulting down upon us. No greeting cards have been gotten out—the photograph for them not yet even made. Yesterday I managed finally to get a tree. Last night, in a snatched hour, we decorated it.

We asked our daughters what was on their Christmas lists. There hadn't been time to make lists, they said. But surely, we insisted, they must have an idea or two in mind. "I'll try to think about it," one of them said. *"Rest,"* said the other. "Mostly I just want rest."

So that's what it has come to, this crazy, incoherent and exhausting time we call a holiday. And we're no busier, no more pressed, than any other family—just stumbling, all of us, through the tyranny of our days, strangers to repose, dead to expectation, having quite forgotten what it's like to be at ease.

Sometimes I have a kind of daydream.

The ring of creditors has finally closed and relieved us of the encumbrance of our goods. My employer has decided he can do nicely without my services. My wife has abandoned her business. The school is finished with our children, or they with it. For whatever reason, the process that leads through fatigue and terror to the ultimate perfection of young minds has been given up, and henceforth they will have to seek knowledge by less brutal means.

We have taken leave of friends, giving them small remembrances, notes of affection and a promise that one day, if we think of it, we will send them an address.

We are in the car, the four of us and our many animals and the few things in suitcases and boxes that we especially want to keep, and the car is pointed along a late afternoon road toward some destination that only we know about. In my imagination, it is a mountain place—a cabin with dark pines around it. And a stack of wood for the fire. And a meadow of snow that awaits, in unhurried patience, the certainty of spring.

"How long before we get there?" one of them asks, in the old habit of making schedules.

"Only as long as it takes," I answer.

"Where will we stop tonight?"

"Anywhere it suits us to."

"And when we get where we're going, how will we pass the time?"

"Selfishly," I say. "Mainly just talking. Being together. With practice, I think we can remember how it's done."

"Will we stay a long time?"

"As long as we're happy there."

"But won't we ever come back?"

"Sure, if we want to. When we're ready."

The car fills up with slow, easy sighs. People and creatures are curled together on the edge of untroubled sleep. But I am wide awake, serene yet absolutely untired. As night comes on, the lights of the machine lead ahead along the unrolling road. Something wonderful is beginning, and there is no timetable to keep.

That is my daydream of simplicity, and it will never come to pass. But, like my daughter whose one wish in this season is for a bit of rest, just being able from time to time to imagine it is the gift I give myself. And it's the only one I need.

78. Comfort Has Its Price

At first light they are waiting on the wire, huddled small inside their feathers, eyes fixed on the door. Jay and sparrow, junco and cardinal, ungainly starling— all made beggars by the snow and by their hunger.

In men or birds, hunger is the great leveler.

From the wire, from the rail of the fence and from their perch in a low, leafless bush, they will watch the door an hour. If it opens, and the woman comes out with a can of seed, they will hurry to be saved. If she forgets, or is gone away somewhere, they will flutter coldly on to other houses, other doors. And if all the doors remain shut, if no one appears to feed them and the snow and cold last, they will perish. A country bird has wider opportunities. But a city bird is charity's prisoner, hostage to a will beyond his own.

Inside the windows of the house are the cats, looking out. The same woman who feeds birds also keeps cats. The cats watch the birds, and the birds, between their peckings at the seed, watch the cats looking at them. The cats are mostly indoor cats, and have rarely caught a bird. They know birds only through the glass. But they know the *uses* of birds, just as birds know the *intentions* of cats. What neither knows is how alike their situations are.

Because the cats' food bowls at that early hour also are empty. If the woman, after coming in from the birds, should forget the cats, hunger would begin to gnaw.

174

The barn cat, like the country bird, can improvise. He can prowl the hayloft for a nest of mice, or hunt the road ditches in the frozen dark. He might ache from bedding in cold places, or wear notched ears from disputes with other ruffians of his kind. But he survives by his wit, and he knows the holes where supper lives. The house cat is a mendicant. Maybe there is a mouse in the basement, and maybe not. If there is, maybe some old memory will remind him how to catch it. And after that one mouse, what?

The house cat looks at the woman as she feeds the birds. Then he looks at his own empty bowl. And at the other cats, looking at *their* empty bowls. What if the house should be silent for a long time? What if footsteps were to cease, and the rattle of the food box were not to be heard again? Ever.

A humiliating anxiety fills them all.

The woman never forgets. Until now, at least, she never has. But that's the danger of being a dependent thing, a *kept* thing—whether you're a bird trained to the feeder, or a house cat trained to the hum of an electric can opener. Or a wage worker, trained by a lifetime's habit in some other man's employ. Everything has its price. And the price of the comfort of letting yourself be kept is, in the end, an awful insecurity.

I think of that whenever I read of some company failing, and its people being flung out unwarned and unprepared into the jobless world. In those times I envy the country bird and the barn cat, hunting the tunnels of the high grass, plucking the wild seed, taking their chances—owing nothing and expecting nothing, living by an art that, past a certain age, is hard to learn.

79. *The Substitute White Cat*

A fill-in was all he was, a substitute white cat to occupy the space left suddenly in a house that was used to having one.

"He's white, is he?" we asked. "We'll take him, then." Aside from the color, we weren't particular. A cat like the one we'd just lost you don't replace. You only try to plug the hole with something white.

So the new one arrived, fresh from a street brawl. He'd been a drifter, the folks who brought him said—shunted from place to place. And he would take no prize for looks. His coat, though white as promised, was coarse and rough. His face, swollen on one side, was cut and crusted from the latest encounter. The other cats of the house took one look at the battered thug and began to sing their cat song of terror and indignation.

He looked at them out of his good eye, the other being mattered nearly shut. He was unimpressed by their singing. He didn't retreat—just fixed them with that one-eyed stare that seemed to say, "It's your move. But I'm warning you, I've been worked over by experts."

We had a sudden vision of weeks, possibly years, spent refereeing cat disputes.

"Maybe we won't keep him," one of us said. "We might have to get rid of him." Though finding a home for anything that looked like that would not be easy. We confined him a week in the upstairs bedroom. The other cats came to sing their rage under the crack of the closed door. He healed, looked more presentable. And feeling better, he came out from under the table and claimed a chair.

The previous white cat, Oliver, had been the third in a line of kings. But this one was a peasant. We tried the old name a time or two, and couldn't make it fit. So we didn't give him any name at all. When anyone had to speak of him, he was just "the new one" or "the white one."

Then the door was left accidentally ajar, and out he came. He found the food bowls on the counter where the others ate. Both eyes open now, he directed his green stare at the dogs, deciding they were neutral. He went where he pleased. The other cats gradually sang less when they saw him. Sometimes they forgot to sing at all.

Eventually, because life is a game of calculated risks, he rolled on his back in front of the black cat, put out a paw. The black one, startled, a bit unsure, put out his own. And like small boys wrestling they tumbled happily across the rug. After that, the singing all but stopped.

"Teddy," my wife said one day. "What do you think of Teddy for a name? He looks a little like a bear." So that was settled.

He liked having a house of his own. He quickly learned to come to lap, to sit on the newspaper as it was being read. He didn't mind not being called by that other name, or that his manner wasn't as kingly or his fur quite as soft as some remembered cat's had been. It didn't matter that he was just a peasant. Because he knew now that his name was Teddy, and he understood that finally he was home.

80. Cold Camp

The house dark. The street dark. The hum of the furnace stilled. All of us—the dog, the cats, the people—struck motionless as statues by the sudden failing of the light.

Somewhere a cable had shorted. All along the block, and several other blocks, the drafts of a frozen night came fingering under the doors and prying at the window cracks of rooms where, only a moment earlier, comfort had been. It is astonishing how quickly a dwelling place goes cold, once the dark has claimed it. The walls we build to separate ourselves from Nature are very costly. But they are very thin.

Once, years ago, when we were new in our house, the ice of a winter storm dragged down the wires and interrupted life for most of four days. The first night we slept under blankets in our own beds, only a little chilly. In the morning, we supposed, the problem would be fixed. It wasn't though.

We built a fireplace fire and soon burned all the dry wood on hand. The rest was in a stack in the yard, some of it left by the last occupant, old wood full of bugs and beginning to go punky. The stack was sheathed under an inch of ice. The pieces had to be chopped out singly and carried in to drain beside the hearth. The thermometer in the hall recorded our progressive losses.

At first the fire warmed the whole room and part of the room beyond. Then the comfort zone grew smaller, until finally it had shrunk to a semicircle extending out two steps, no more, from the fireplace itself. By afternoon of the second day, the thermometer stood at 50 degrees. By morning of the next, it registered only a little more than 40.

178

People of some neighborhoods went off to rest warm in hotel beds, and the empty houses of some of them were burgled meantime. Under our roof there was nothing to interest a discriminating thief. But, having lived there only three months, we were too stubborn to let ourselves be driven out. Our daughters were small, then. Small enough that the four of us could fit together, crowded close enough for common warmth, inside a double sleeping bag.

By day we wore all our heaviest sweaters and coats and tended the fire and observed the thermometer, commenting on its steady fall. The kitchen stove was gas, so we were able to cook and keep warm cups in hand. By night we lighted our central room with candles, and read by a camping lantern, and told winter stories—storm stories—that were told us by the generation before. And when fatigue drugged us all, which was early in that temperature, we stoked up the fire with dry wood, unrolled our bag in front of it, crept inside and went quickly, deliciously off to sleep, all closely touching.

I can't say how long we might have held out against the cold. Although I like to think now that, given food enough and firewood enough, we could have made it through to spring. In any case, that wasn't necessary. The fourth morning, at some small hour, we awoke in a frightful sweat, the fire burning high, the furnace throbbing and radiators hot to the touch, every light bulb in the house ablaze.

And as quickly as this telling of it, almost without any comment, life resumed its safe and uneventful march.

Then, several evenings ago, the lights went out again, though only briefly—only for a couple of hours. And the cold came probing. One of the cats passed through the room where we were sitting. The creature stopped and stretched, and the candlelight flung its shadow large against the wall. And all those memories came back.

179

I have been astonished by the clarity of the girls'
recollection of those nights, for their ages then were
only 2 and 3. They remember it all: The sense of fine
adventure, the dark hours occupied with stories, the
minding of the fire, the nearness as we slept. Whenever
the lights have flickered on a night of a winter storm,
I have sensed in them—even when sometimes they
have not spoken it—the yearning that we might need
to draw so closly together, to amuse and attend and
comfort one another that way again.

Rarely do we have to. The artificial comfort around
us is wonderfully reliable. Almost always we are safe,
and that's the pity.

81. *Filling In the Blanks*

The snow came softly, wetly, and in the first hour
of morning the world was white.

Rufus woke me, whining for his minute in the yard.
I set the coffee heating, and let him out, then climbed
the stair again with dog and morning cup. As I passed
in the blueness of the hall, her voice came out from
the open door of her room.

"It's so beautiful," she said—meaning, of course, the
wonder of the day. The words startled me, because I
hadn't thought she'd be awake.

So I carried my coffee in, and we looked out together
from her window. Every branch and twig was encased,
each tree a spectral object. The whiteness of lawn and
street, at that early hour, still was perfectly unmarked.
You don't get a snow that wonderful very often.

"It's so beautiful," she said again. And though I
nodded without speaking, what I really felt was a
quick, sharp little ache.

We've been involved, these last weeks, in the ordeal of college applications—a tyranny devised by those citadels of higher knowledge to disfigure, as far as possible, a child's last year at home. It used to be that you picked a school, read the literature, and if it sounded like a more or less congenial place you bought a bus ticket and enrolled there. But all that's changed. Today, no college is considered worth attending unless its application is so complex as to plunge not just the student but the entire family into several months of unremitting anxiety and despair.

That's what we've been about, then—all of us— filling in the blanks on endless sheaves of official-looking documents, watching the calendar days melt away toward a deadline as inflexible and ominous as doom itself. Miss it, and you're condemned to a life on the dole. That is what you're supposed to believe, anyway, and the college gatekeepers have run their bluff with cleverness and great success.

So we've been furiously grappling with the applications. It keeps you busy. Boy, does it keep you busy! Awash in a sea of mindless make-work, you forget the point of it all. You forget what the craziness means.

And that's what I remembered, suddenly, when we were looking out together at the snow from the window of her room. *She's going,* my heart whispered. And for the first time, I think, I really believed it.

The years will turn faster, now. There'll be other snows as fine as this one. But she will see them in different places, through other windows. And that's all right. That's how it's always been, and how it should be. I want her to finish growing up, and her sister after her, and for both of them to have their lives.

But what about me? said a secret voice—a shameful, self-pitying little voice that refused to be stilled. *What will it be like to rise on all those other winter mornings, and let the dog out, and make my coffee, then climb the stair and pass along the hall, past those*

181

doors from which no voices ever speak an invitation to share the magic of the day?

"Do you remember our snowmen?" she asked then.

I told her I remembered.

"And the sledding hill. We'll sled again sometime, won't we?"

"Sure we will," I said.

We might even have done it that very morning, except that the stack of applications waited and there still was no end to the blanks that had to be filled. Those are the easy ones. The harder blanks to fill will come later.

IV.

82. *Tired Runner*

For the old dog, Cinnamon, this is the 15th winter. Without complaint, but failing almost as we watch, she struggles now to claim the prize of one last spring.

Incontinent of late, stone deaf and nearly sightless, she passes the days closed up in the kitchen, with sun filtering in through the hanging window plants and a familiar rug to lie on. When one of us goes in or out, she lifts her gray mask toward the door to identify, if she can, which of the known shadows that might be.

Once only, in the evening, she ascends the stair, arriving breathless at the top. And she is able still, with effort and some prior hesitation, to negotiate the leap to her accustomed sleeping place at the bottom of the bed. She's welcome, even if eventually we'll have to lift her there.

Along with infirmity, great age has brought with it one small compensation. The thunderstorms that used to srike terror in her soul roll past and on unheard. Whistle, and she responds. She still can hear, intermittently, the buzz of the doorbell. Those are the only sounds that pierce the silence. Sometimes I bend close and, lifting a soft ear, speak a word or two of encouragement. Whether anything registers or not, she seems to appreciate the effort.

Although safe now from the storm's distant drumming, she is prey to some unease whose source we cannot know. Much of the time she sleeps. But, when not sleeping, she paces—endlessly, toenails clicking on the vinyl of the kitchen floor. From rug to food dish, to water bowl, to dish, to rug, then back to dish again. Sometimes in her pacing she is seized by a fit of shuddering so profound that her whole body shakes unsteadily and her teeth can be heard to rattle. Then the spasm passes, and she resumes her clicking march. It could be pain, although she does not whimper or cry out. Or maybe it is some kind of transient waking dream, or presentiment. I hope not pain.

She came, a stray, when our daughters were hardly more than toddlers, and has helped us raise them—defending the door against any evil—until the girls are nearly women. She has welcomed, washed and raised more foundling kittens than most mother cats do in their lifetimes.

Cinnamon always has loved the snow. On the morning after the last blizzard, she whined at the door, and when I opened it she rushed happily out into the drifts. For several moments she gamboled like a pup, rolling in the powder, thrusting her blind, white old face full into it and tunneling like a mole. But afterward, when she started back, her rear legs failed her. She stumbled, and had to sit to regain a bit of strength for the 10-yard journey to the house.

In her younger days, she went with us on outings to the farm and cabin. Then she grew matronly and short of wind. And we stopped taking her, afraid that an immoderate romp in the woods or swim across the pond would cause her heart to stop. Now I regret those missed chances.

If, by luck and will, she lives to see the turn of spring, that's where we'll go together on the first fine day—to that piece of country ground she can see in memory, even after eyes have dimmed. I will lift her ear to break the silence with a shout. And send her running blindly, lamely, through the leaf-fall of all our seasons down the lane behind the cabin. And I will hope the darkness overtakes her just then, in joyous mid-step.

What did we imagine we were saving her for, anyway? Time can't be saved or slowed. Only *wasted*.

83. *Toward Accidental Lives*

My daughter and her classmates have come to that point in their schooling when it is thought that they might usefully begin considering occupations. So, from time to time now, one or another of us parents is brought before them to discuss from personal experience the ways in which it is possible to misspend a life.

Naturally, I speak to them about the trade of newspapering, and about a writer's lot in general—trying not to give the impression of someone who has stumbled through his years in aimlessness and sequential accidents. Trying, that is, to conceal the truth.

Before me, it was a physician father who entertained the class by dissecting a cow's heart, the very witnessing of which may have aborted several potentially brilliant surgical careers. And so it goes. Each of us will have to take his or her turn: Policemen, salespersons, carpenters with fingers missing, accountants made astigmatic by too many cramped columns of numbers, lawyers, pipefitters, gentleman cosmeticians and lady boxers. Until, at last, the whole baffling range of possibilities has been explored.

I don't object a bit to this occasional light duty. The visits are enjoyable enough, and probably do no material harm. But invariably I am struck, looking into those credulous and attentive faces, by how huge a pretense adulthood mostly is and by how little of real importance I have to share.

Part of me sits speaking before the class. Another part stands critically aside a step or two, observing, listening to what is said. Many of those children have come, over the years, to be my friends. I wish that all of them were. But the manner of my speaking to them is not that of a conversation with friends at all.

The words have a ring of authority. Their tone is altogether confident. They draw a line between us. *Listen here,* they seem to say, *it is clear that we are very different. I have lived longer than any of you, and gotten grayer, and therefore I have come to know a great many things, all of them true and important. Listen to what I have to tell you, and it may be that you will improve yourselves.*

That is the fraud, of course. And the worst part is that, looking into my young friends' eyes, I can see that this preposterous nonsense is believed. So conditioned are children to accept the power and excellence of adults that almost any fool can appear before them and pass himself off for a sage.

What I hear myself telling them is not what I would really want to say, if I had the courage. I'd speak in a quieter voice—maybe in that solemn whisper they use to transmit the secrets of their own lives. And it would have nothing to do with how some job is done, mine or anyone else's.

Almost everything is a confusion, I would openly confess, or something to that effect. *And anyone who tells you differently is not to be believed. I remember myself sitting at that school desk where you're sitting now—my books and papers and my thoughts as cluttered as yours are. Or maybe worse. Well, that clutter stays with you. Growing up clarifies nothing.*

The confusion remains, and may even increase. The skills you learn will be useful or not. Ambition may serve you well or poorly. All that is yet to be seen. What's certain is that some very distant day, looking back across an eternity of accidents, you will find yourself unchanged in any profound way from who you are just now. So obey us adults because you must. But believe in our great wisdom at your own risk.

That's what I'd say to them if I ever dared. And likely never be invited back to school again.

84. *A Cosmic Yawn*

The low level of interest in comet-watching seems to me conclusive evidence that, as a nation, we are losing the science race to the Japanese, the Russians and the South Sandwich Islanders.

Other nations sent spacecraft out to visit Halley's comet, take pictures and collect samples. The United States couldn't afford to. Now this cosmic event of a lifetime has come and gone. And my daughters' school, which will travel to the end of the known universe to play a basketball game, didn't consider the comet worth a field trip to a hill on the edge of town.

So when I heard a radio announcer say, one recent night, that the next morning would be about the last good chance for viewing Halley's, I suggested we make a family outing of it.

"You can bet the Japanese will be out," I told my children. "They'll all take turns taking pictures of each other taking pictures of the comet. The simultaneous snapping of their Nikon lenses will be recorded on seismographs as far away as Montevideo. The Russians will get all their collective farmers out of bed in the middle of the night and make them stand on top of crates of sugar beets for as long as it takes to prove the superiority of Soviet eyesight. Anyone who doesn't see Halley's will be classified as crazy and will receive an injection."

"What about the South Sandwich Islanders?" my daughters asked, charmed by the name.

"They live 37 degrees below the equator," I explained. "So for them it's easy. They can just pack a picnic basket and sit on the beach, eating their south sandwiches and watching the comet go more or less overhead. For us here in the Northern Hemisphere it's harder. Halley's will only be visible above the southern horizon for a short time in the early morning."

"How early?"

"Four o'clock," I told them. "But to get far enough from the lights of the city, we ought to be up by about half past two. Three at the latest." I sensed an immediate reduction in their curiosity about comets.

"Maybe we'll catch it next time around," one of them said.

"Sure," I told them, trying not to show my disappointment. "It's up to you. However, I am a man in my 50s, so I intend to set the alarm for 2:30 in the morning." And I meant to.

That night we had friends in from out of town who wanted to hear some jazz. We got a table five feet from the band. The good sounds washed over us. Time passed. I woke up with the Sunday morning sun streaming through the window onto the bed. One of the girls looked in at the bedroom door.

"You missed it," she said.

"Missed it *nothing!*" I replied alertly. "It was fabulous."

"Really? Like what?"

"Well, there was this terrific bright light that lit up the whole sky. The best part, though, was the tail, which was like a fiery rainbow in all different colors— blue, green, magenta, puce—stretching almost from horizon to horizon. I suppose nothing like it was ever seen before."

"Sounds neat."

"Once in a lifetime," I told her.

In the absence of any initiative by the schools, it's up to education in the home to close the science gap.

85. *Sorry, He's Unavailable*

He was an exceptional cat. Even sprawled in a busy intersection, stunned by the wheel or bumper of a car, his excellence was apparent. In another minute or so, however, he was apt to be a good deal flatter and less exceptional.

So my wife, who has a sharp eye for livestock, collected him from the street and brought him home. That's how they've come to us, all but one of them, by some accident or other. Except for the law and the neighbors, there's no upper limit on the number we would keep. The others demonstrate for a day or two, then move aside and make room. The household stabilizes again. And we settle back to await the next accident, the next boarder.

This one was no alley cat, though. He was sleek as a seal and, after the trauma of the street had passed, was wonderfully gentle. What's more, there'd been some financial investment in him, of the kind you make when you like cats but think their population ought to be finite. So someone had cared about him. And someone might be missing him.

We advertised in the classified columns. As happened once before the ad generated an obscene call. We again were charmed that there are people who organize their day's indecent whisperings around the lost-animal ads in the newspaper. There is a case for neutering, all right, and not just of cats. There also were two or three legitimate calls, although after that first one we answered the phone less civilly. Those people described their lost cats. We described the one we had. Always he was the wrong cat. The callers sounded a bit put out that we had advertised, but probably they were only disappointed.

By this time, several days had passed and the cat still was in the back room, still apart from the others who knew that he was there but pretended they didn't notice. Not wanting to excite the whisperer with another classified ad, I put a notice on the office bulletin board. I work with some strange people, and what they say over the telephone is their own affair. But at least, I thought, the offer of a cat would not inflame them to lewdity.

I was wrong. Some of their comments, on reading the notice about the cat, were very coarse indeed. Most just ignored it. I enlarged on the note, restating the offer in language a bit more florid.

And I discovered a principle. If you ever want to know a lot about your colleagues—their allergies, the cramped size of their apartments and so forth—just put up a note about a cat. They'll tell you everything. Everyone has an excuse, and the excuses range from new Oriental carpets to killer parakeets.

Not to prolong the suspense, an associate at the office did finally take the creature. Or, rather, his mother did. She happened to be visiting from several hundred miles away. But he persuaded her to have a look and, like my wife, she is a fine judge of catflesh. Her previous cat had been fed a daily ration of liver and yeast and had lived 27 years before dying in her lap. Our lodger rode away with her in the car, to a home on a shady street in a quiet town, not even beginning to suspect yet what a deal he'd fallen into.

Quick as Shadows Passing

So, to the posted notice, I added a bulletin saying the cat was gone. Immediately people began coming out of the office woodwork—a lot of them.

I knew someone who wanted that cat of yours, they'd say. Or, *He sounded like a hell of a cat, that one did.* Or, *I'd made up my mind to take him. I was going to tell you in about an hour.* Their expressions were heavy with disappointment and reproach.

Thus was revealed a second principle: If you ever want to know the intensity of your friends' devotion to cats, just let it be known discreetly that they've missed their chance.

86. Discovering the Wheel

One daughter has passed instantly from crib to early adulthood. The other is following only a year behind. And the automotive pressure shows signs of getting fierce.

In television ads, the birthday girl rushes expectantly to her window on that magic morning, draws aside the chintz curtain and sees, parked on the drive below, a sparkling new machine, usually red, that announces her coming of age.

With a yelp of pleasure, she flies downstairs to receive the keys from Daddy—a cartoon of beaming indulgence, but nonetheless seeming now to be more provident and less stupid than he seemed the night before. Then she goes out for a trial spin in this gift that will make her the envy of any friends who, unlike her, have not yet achieved their vehicular majority.

I don't know how the idea got started that, like voices changing and bosoms appearing, the possession of a car is just one more part of the organic process of growing up. In our house, that is now seen to be a cruel misunderstanding.

The birthday girl leapt from bed and ran to her window, drew up the shade (there are no chintz curtains at the window, much less red Porsches on the drive). When she looked out, what she saw was the family station wagon with seven circumferences of the Earth on its odometer. She did not fly downstairs into my arms. That's perfectly all right. I am not so insecure that I have to buy my children's respect with automobiles.

Things were chilly for a day or two. Then, at dinner, I said to her, "Well, you're 18 now." She looked at her plate. It must be terrible to be reminded that you are 18 without anything to drive. Like finding out Mister Right has given you a paste engagement ring.

"I have some news for you," I said.

Hope flickered faintly.

"There's a typewriter in your future."

"Great."

"An electric typewriter," I said. "With automatic correction, if you want it."

"Terrific. All the options."

She didn't seem to understand the significance of my announcement, so I launched into a brief soliloquy whose purpose was to establish the importance of typewriters and fix their place in history and contemporary affairs.

I explained that while most people in the world take automobiles pretty much for granted, typewriters are instruments of real power and thus widely feared. For example, you cannot frighten a Russian with a Ford, a Datsun or even a Minuteman missile. But typewriters, and the uses that can be made of them, give Soviet party hacks the heebie-jeebies.

Several months ago, I recalled, I had to go into an African country run by a moderately demented dictator. His minions at the airport weren't the least interested in anything else I was carrying, but my

196

Olympia portable with a nonfunctioning E scared them out of their wits. They took it away from me and all stood in a circle around it like a bomb squad around a ticking box, looking at it with awe and bafflement. I had to argue like crazy to get it back.

That's the kind of power a typewriter has, alongside which hardly any other machine can even be compared. A car is really only a short step up from the horse and wagon. It may get you there a little faster, a little easier. But in the right hands, a typewriter can change the world.

"Maybe you should take a typing course this summer," I suggested.

"How about driver's ed?" she countered, leading me to think possibly the issue is not closed.

87. *The Jungle Time*

Morning is the jungle time. Through the back door and into the early light they come boiling all together, shoving and shouldering like a football team coming out of the locker room. It must be an electric moment for the smaller wildlife of the yard.

The black cat goes directly for the dark tangle of bushes beside the fence, vanishing in the shadow. The bird dog stylishly points a tree in whose higher reaches he has spied an impudent squirrel. The white cat, after rolling in the dust, imagines himself camouflaged and settles in plain view to wait for a feeble-minded chipmunk. The gray cat climbs a tree to the garage roof, explores to a corner of the eave, forgets the way back and sets up a pitiful wailing.

Each morning it's the same. They are trying to remember the wild things they used to be. But it's no good.

The squirrel is sure-footed. He peers down bright-eyed from his branch. In the darkness of the bushes nothing moves. The chipmunk watches safe from his hole, knowing a dirty white cat is no more trustworthy than a clean one. Birds long ago gave up nesting in the trees of a yard where upturned green stares await the fledgling generations. So nothing is gotten, ever.

But that morning hour powerfully stirs their imaginations. Then the woman of the house comes outside and calls their names, and spoils everything. There's nothing left except to play the hiding game. But it's useless if you're white. And no fun at all if you're frightened on a roof. And lonesome if the others have all gone inside and you're left alone in the empty bushes.

The primal memories recede, replaced by other thoughts: Of the rattle of food going from sack into dish; of the sound of milk being poured, or of the machine as it opens a tuna can. The sun already is above the trees. The early haze is gone, and the jungle is just a yard again. Soon the spring warmth will bear down. They are thinking of cool rooms, of cushions, of the day's activity in the kitchen and the lucky accidents that sometimes flow from that.

After their quarter-hour of liberty, they gladly come in.

Then, in the long march of the day, as they peer out through the glass, the idea slowly reforms itself. Did something move there in the foliage? See the fatness of that noisy jay! Could tomorrow be the day the squirrel errs and falls?

All through the silent night the fever builds. And in the morning, when the radio plays and the people stir, they are waiting together at the door, eager to crowd through, to rush outside and resume the hunt for something in themselves—something they misplaced an age ago, and cannot now quite remember.

88. The Sounds of Lives Together

The piano exercise they are mastering now is a piece by Beethoven. The lilt of it sweetly fills the house during most idle minutes of the day. And though some of the chords occasionally confound them, the music they make—even such imperfect music—comes as a miracle to one whose own fingers always were like great, numb loaves of sausage on the keys.

The instrument they play is an ancient upright, painted black. I remember how I shuddered when it came into our lives, fearing there might not be room enough under one roof for me and the hymns of discord, endlessly repeated. That concern was unnecessary. For the capacity of a house is not absolute. Within reason, the space has a way of expanding to accommodate whatever new creature or activity is introduced.

Very soon, then, as always happens, the notes of the piano had merged into the larger and indiscriminate sound of our lives together. That sound is like a tapestry, and it is composed of many threads which are detected singly only if one deliberately commands the ear to separate them out.

Just now, for example, besides the Beethoven, a rhythmic thumping can be heard. I do not know how long it has been going on, since I grew used to it long ago and it seldom registers anymore. It is the sound of a tennis ball striking the door of the garage. One daughter—the one not seated at the piano—is playing some solitary game out there on a cloudy afternoon.

From a different quarter of the house comes, more faintly, the whistle of the tea kettle. I know its meaning exactly. My wife intends to pour a cup and sit a few quiet moments—well, not quiet, exactly, but private ones—with the day's paper before shouldering again the millstone of our punctual hunger.

Nearer at hand there is an insistent scratching. What possibly could be making such a racket? Why, it's the old dog, of course! Seeking sanctuary from Rufus's teasing, she has gone under a bureau and, in her fatness, gotten wedged there.

As for me, I produce a typewriter's clicking which the others, except for the stuck dog, are not close enough to hear. But even if they were, probably they would not notice it, since that is my customary background noise.

These are the threads which, taken all together— these and numberless routine sounds like them— provide the subtle announcement that the fabric is intact, that we are still, for a little while longer, all together. One recent weekend morning I found myself, shortly after waking, unaccountably depressed. There was nothing, no sadness or distress that I could put a name to. Only a curious sense of loss and vacancy as I made ready to set out upon the day.

Then I realized that something was missing. Not *something*. One of the girls had spent the night at a friend's house. And in her absence, her sister, too, was sleeping late. The stillness was deeply affecting.

The lack of their sounds—the empty place where their voices and their rustlings should have been—left a cavity that the traffic on the street outside and the barkings of early dogs could not begin to fill. And I was struck by how much I have come to depend on the accidental noises of them about—the percussion of garage door, the splash of water in tub or sink, even the cannon fire of their occasional wars—for proof that my world is in order and the household complete.

These separations have greatly increased in frequency. Soon they will be habit. Until finally, depending on geography and circumstance and the turns that lives can take, the black piano will fall permanently silent and this apartness will become our natural condition.

That's as it should be. It is the same for all creatures that raise their young, invariably to give them up. I do not rail against it, but neither would I care to hurry it. Nor could I pretend, that recent silent morning, to have at all enjoyed the rehearsal.

89. *Verse Won't Rhyme with Purse*

"All right," I told the one who wants to be a poet. "If your heart's set on it, I won't stand in the way." I do not want her to pass through life, bitter at somehow being deflected from her destiny. "But you need to have a plan," I said. "We all have to eat."

"Of course I'll eat."

"I didn't say, You. I said *We*. If you're going to be a poet, I want you to marry well."

"That's ridiculous," she said.

"No, I'm dead serious. We'll shift our investment out of education and into cosmetics, clothes and charm school. A poet's life can be cruel. The important thing is to keep your nerve and your figure, and look for someone with deep pockets." That was not sexist prattle. I would have given exactly the same advice to a poetic son.

As we talked, I was reminded a little resentfully about the way that children, in choosing their careers, tend to be so indifferent to their parents' later needs. Having kids costs a lot. I have not run the numbers through a calculator. Nor am I the kind of father who would put an exact price on every pair of shoes, every jar of applesauce or pureed carrots, every stuffed toy. Some things—birthday cakes, for example—I would not count at all. They are gifts of love.

But the fact remains that child rearing is a pricey affair. Suppose, just to pick a figure out of the air, that it costs $100,000 to nurture a child from the cradle to the threshold of real earning power. And suppose that child becomes a doctor.

I do not, at the moment, require a physician's services very often. But as great age comes on, I plan to be sick a lot. Or at least to spend quite a bit of time malingering and getting sympathy. Say that, beginning in my 70th year, I visited the doctor on average once a week. At $50 an office call, I would only have to live 38 more years—or until age 108 and about five months—before recovering my entire investment.

That is if the doctor were my own child. If it's somebody else's child, the money's just gone like smoke.

The same calculation could be done for any number of other fixed expenses. The accountant who works our taxes usually presents a bill for somewhere in the neighborhood of $500. I admit it would take staying power, but by age 270, if the kid were a CPA, I'd have gotten every dime back.

The barber asks $11.50 for a haircut and beard trim, and I go to him once a month, whether or not there's anything there to cut. That comes to $138 a year. In other words, a tonsorially gifted child could, in just under 725 years, amortize himself free and clear.

But when, I ask, was the last time you heard of parents being supported in their golden years by a *poet?* By the time their young are fledged, mothers and fathers usually are plucked clean and incapable of flight. In fairness, then, it should be the offsprings' turn to bring home the worm.

Poems, unfortunately, cannot be confused with worms.

90. *Despite the Odds*

For the last 100 to 150 million years, give or take a few million, birds—or something like them—have been leaving the nest to make their way in a changing world. Was it always in late spring that they began their journey? Or, in that warmer age, did seasons even matter?

A paleozoologist would know the answer, but I do not. I only know that every year, in this time of risk and small tragedies, I am driven again to wonder how much practice is enough. If, after at least a million centuries of trying, the birds haven't yet got it right, can they ever? Or can we?

The other afternoon, the bird dog, Rufus, was transfixed by something in the window well. His posture was midway between a point and a pounce. Plainly he was interested in what was down there, but also a bit confused. So I put him in his pen and went back to investigate.

Down in the farthest corner of the well, standing perfectly straight and still, its back against the dusty glass like some prisoner at the execution wall, waiting for the shot, was a nestling jay. Slate-colored and not yet fully feathered, it had tumbled from a branch and found its way, somehow, to that sheltered place. Would it find its way out again? Would the parent birds come to feed it there during the several days more before it gained the prize of flight?

The one certain thing, confirmed by failed mercies from boyhood onward, was that my intervention would be useless. According to the literature, most song-birds—of which the jay is one, though its song may be raucous and unpleasing—quit the nest before they have mastered the use of their wings. For a brief but critical time, then, they are vulnerable.

The creature would make it or would not, according to some law I hadn't written and couldn't change. And when I looked in the window well the next morning, the little jay was dead.

A few evenings later we were eating out on an outdoor deck at the home of friends when a clamor arose from the edge of the yard. The people's dog, small and inoffensive, had strayed too near the bushes where, evidently, an immature robin was hiding. Adult robins swarmed and darted at the dog in noisy defense.

In past years, for a time, we kept a wren house hanging. Sweetly the wrens would trill their song of courtship. Industriously they brought straws and grass, and later seeds and bugs, to the hole in the box. Then, one day, the young would clamber forth and drop clumsily from the perch. And likely as not a cat was waiting. Or something was. And because even the smallest sorrows can be cumulatively unbearable, we let the wren house fall from the tree and never put it back.

So I think of the birds, and of their bad planning. And, because it is the season when the young of our own kind also are going out—and with less practice; not with 100 million years' experience, but a mere 3 million or even only 500,000, depending on how you reckon—I think of them as well.

Immense the dangers are, and disheartening the casualties. There are no promises; there never have been. Bird parents or human ones, we invest the whole capital of our longer future in them—then send them out, never safe and not quite fully made, to try their luck against the unimagined ill that waits.

But look around you. Despite the odds, the miracle repeats.

91. The World's Bravest Man

Human flies have climbed 70-story buildings without the aid of ropes. Men have gone over Niagara Falls in a barrel, launched themselves across canyons on jet-powered motorcycles, spent the night in pits filled with vipers, caught bullets between their teeth.

These are cheap stunts by exhibitionists of only moderate nerve, and they do not greatly impress me anymore, now that I have met one of the truly bravest people in the world.

The other afternoon I took my younger daughter for her driver's examination. The written test she had passed earlier. This was the practical exam. She was instructed to park the car on the drive beside the building, headed toward the exit of the parking lot, and wait for an examiner.

"I'm nervous," she said.

"Relax," I told her. "The worst that can happen is you might fail, and have to take it again." In certain circumstances, a small lie like that is justified.

Presently, a slender man in uniform emerged from the office and strode toward the car. The nameplate he wore identified him as Examiner Thomas. His eyes were very clear and wonderfully alert. He walked with that easy, swinging carriage of someone—a bomb dismantler, perhaps, or an old-time gunfighter—who has seen so much danger that what would terrify the rest of us no longer has the same meaning for him.

"Ready to go, Jennifer Sue?" he asked in a gentle voice. She nodded that she was. And while I watched, the two of them set off together into the maelstrom of the street.

That's when my thoughts turned to the incredible courage of Examiner Thomas and his colleagues. Teaching one's own child to drive is a harrowing experience. But these are people who get up every morning, knowing they will spend the day riding in cars operated by beginners who may still be unclear about the difference between the accelerator and the brake.

"How long does the test take?" I asked the man inside the office.

"About 12 minutes," he said. "If everything goes well."

"And if it doesn't, what's the hospital of preference?"

He laughed. "Anywhere they can stop the internal bleeding."

I went back outside and waited for the car to reappear, which shortly it did, both riders still whole.

"She has a couple of things she needs to work on," Examiner Thomas reported. "But she passed the test." He got out with his clipboard, as cool and unruffled as someone who'd spent his life behind a desk.

I had to ask him: "Does anyone ever have a wreck during the test?"

He skewered me with those clear eyes—as if I'd maybe stood too long uncovered in the sun. It was a stupid question, like asking an animal trainer if the tiger really has teeth.

"Do you see that third door down?" He nodded toward the row of shops in which the license office was housed. "A woman drove through the front of that building with me in the car," said Examiner Thomas. Then he went inside to get the papers on the next testee.

Show-offs and professional daredevils get all the ink. But this world is full of genuine heroes whose praises are seldom sung.

92. How Teddy Measures Time

The white cat, Teddy, has taken on a fearful lot of weight. It's the result, I think, not so much of gluttony as of a kind of basic confusion about how time passes. He mistakes the minutes for hours, meaning that the interval between meals is greatly shortened. And the effect can be seen in other things as well.

Each morning he joins the crowd of his fellow household creatures, gathered for the jostling rush through the back door out into the dewy wilderness of the yard. His anticipation of that moment obviously is keen.

It isn't a lengthy outing—a part of an hour, only. But all the others stay out until they are called. A couple of the more adventurous have to be retrieved manually. Not Teddy. Eyes shining, stubby little legs churning, he heaves himself out into the natural world. But in the half-minute it takes to fill the coffeepot and set it heating, he's back again, the novelty of exploring already worn off.

Anxiously he peers at the closed door, wondering whether he's been forgotten. He gives the impression of someone who's spent the whole day abroad, and is worried about night catching him a long way from nourishment.

Let inside, he goes directly to his food bowl. Then he watches the others through the window. And in another couple of minutes it occurs to him that the morning has gotten long, and that it must be lunch time. It's little errors like that, in men or cats, that cause the waist to disappear.

He came to us from hard times, Teddy did. His great round face was stitched and scarred, and there'd been spells when the meals weren't so regular. His change of luck, when it came, may simply have been too sudden and comprehensive to fully grasp. One moment he was a battered refugee, growling to hide his terror, slitted eyes casting around for a threat. The next minute there were cushions and catnip on a newspaper on the kitchen floor. And there were benign dogs. And a good-humored cat who never showed a claw was inviting him to play.

People took him up and stroked him. A girl creature smoothed his coat with a brush. Strangers arriving at the door saw him and pronounced an unexpected word: *Beautiful!* And if all that change could occur almost in an eye blink, why wouldn't his whole concept of hours and days be much compressed?

Whenever something nice happens, he celebrates— as any of us would—by rushing off to get a tasty bite. Which would be fine, if those were occasional events. But nice things happen too often. His celebrations are practically continuous.

If you ask me, good luck has permanently disordered the way that Teddy measures time. Woolly coated, broad-backed, solid as a steer, he waddles among us now, covered in great rolls of happiness. *There's not a dark cloud anywhere in sight,* you almost can see him thinking. And immediately he feels an appetite coming on.

93. *The Caldwell Eyebrow*

I do not suppose for a minute that the Caldwell eyebrow ever will take its place in literature and medical history alongside the lisps, clawed hands and hemophilia of certain of the European royal families. But it is a trait as pronounced as any of those. And for whatever small credit it may be worth, I can claim to be the first to have observed and described it.

There hangs on our bedroom wall a photograph of several women of the last century—seven sisters of the Caldwell side of my wife's family, arranged three in front and four behind for a formal portrait.

At various times the picture has been stored under beds and in closets. But for the last two or three years it has been displayed, mainly, as I remember, because of the attractiveness of the carved frame. When the photograph was made I cannot say. Although, counting back three generations, it must have been in the late 1860s or early 1870s.

The look of these seven sisters is not—how to say this delicately—either very warm or winning. I would judge them to range in age between about 16 and 27 or 28, ordinarily soft and charming years. But they all have put on rather severe expressions for the occasion. Perhaps that was the convention for photos of the day. Their hair styles, too, are severe, parted in the center and caught up in a high bun behind. Nor is the period dress particularly becoming—puffed shoulders, balloon sleeves, high choker collars and stiff fronts, brocaded and starched. Four of the seven display some sort of identical watch or large locket affixed high on the bosom, just inside the shoulder.

The photograph once was richly tinted. But the artist's colors have faded over these hundred years and more, especially from the faces. So the immediate effect—the costumes, the sepulchral pallor of those features so grimly set—is of a picture that might be found hanging on a study wall in some unoccupied castle in Transylvania.

The girl on the left in the front row is my wife's grandmother. And the one on the right, in the back, whom I would guess to be the youngest, can be seen at a closer look to be quite beautiful, very tiny and wasp-waisted, although it is reported that she became elephantine in the later years of her life.

For some months I felt an indefinable unease in the presence of that picture. There was about it something subtly disturbing—something that challenged the idle viewer. It was as if the photograph had made a statement and was waiting now, had been waiting lifetimes, for a response. Then one day I noticed. It was a quality in the faces of the ladies. Something about their eyes. No—their eyebrows. And specifically the right eyebrow.

Either in fact or by some accident of shadow, it appeared markedly more prominent than the left one. What's more—and this was no trick of light—that right brow was sharply arched. Of the seven girls in the picture, six exhibited the characteristic quite strikingly, the seventh not at all. It was as though their brows had been drawn up and affixed with tape. To the affected ones, it gave an oddly quizzical expression, a look of penetrating disdain. Or was it something else and worse?

In any event, this seemed to have been a common feature among the antique ladies of that line. One could imagine generations of Caldwell women scuttling through the gorse of the Scottish highlands and, later, along the first rude lanes of the New England colonies, the right brows of all of them asking the same silent question of the world.

Then I put it out of mind.

Until, several weeks later, I happened off-handedly to glance at another picture on that wall, this one a photo of my wife. The realization struck me like a fist, and what was amazing was that I had not noticed sooner. She had the Caldwell eyebrow.

Quickly I got out the scrapbooks and searched through them for pictures of my daughter, the one who most favors her mother. I examined five years of school photographs. And is it necessary to tell you? Of course the feature was there. My understanding of genetics is slight. But I seem to have read somewhere that the heritable tendencies a parent transmits to a child are not susceptible to compromise. That is, the genes pass intact—then manifest their results or not, depending on their dominance and the characteristics the other parent brings to the union.

The Caldwell eyebrow, it appears, is carried by a very powerful gene. It does not cause the bearer to be locked away in the tower or disqualified for coronation, if coronation were the issue. But it will be loose among us until this affected branch of the Caldwell tree happens finally to wither away in barrenness. A very extensive branch it must now be. For there are seven sisters in that picture, and six are marked.

Coldly they stare out from behind the glass. Arch and sardonic, and wholly in control. *"Do you think he has noticed?"* they are silently asking. That is the question in their eyes.

"Who can be sure?" answers my wife, from her frame beside them on the wall.

And then my daughter, from a page of the open scrapbook: *"I believe not yet."*

94. Is the Doctor In?

Youth moves with a quick, sure stride, hardly noticing that the Earth is revolving underfoot at something over 1,000 miles an hour. But let enough years pass and the trick gets harder. The steps of age are as halting as of an infant just beginning.

Life being a circular affair, it appears that we will once more be spending quite a lot of time visiting on the telephone with the Poison Control Center. The number used to be taped to the wall beside the phone desk in the kitchen. We'll have to put it up again.

Our daughters, in their early years, were omnivores. The medicines we kept locked inside a cabinet, but there was plenty of other stuff to eat. For salad, there were the leaves of semi-toxic house plants. When autumn added color to the menu, they were attracted to the fat orange berries of bittersweet. One of the girls would come smiling blissfully, with crumbs of something horrid on her lips, and we would ring up our friends at the poison center to have another nice conversation about stomach pumps and ipecac.

The experts there are very thorough. They read from the literature as they speak to you on the phone. *"How much of it did she eat? Are her pupils dilated? Is she alert? Is her speech affected?"* Drastic measures never were required. Our girls were connoisseurs, tasting samples only. As soon as they were of an age to understand the meaning of a stomach pump, and how one works, their grazing on the household vegetation ended. The hazard passed, and we took the number down.

The other morning, though, my wife was on the phone again. It was a strange and early hour, and I wondered who she was calling.

"The veterinarian," she said. "But he doesn't know for sure. And the druggist isn't open yet. We'd better call Poison Control."

"You mean they're at it again?" I cried. The past flashed before me.

"No," she said. "Not the girls. I seem to have taken one of these." She handed me the bottle. It was the dog's medicine, administered daily to prevent something with the awful name of heartworm.

"I got out a pill. And then I made a cup of tea. I was looking out the window at the sunlight and kind of dreaming. I started to drink my tea, and the pill was lying there and—well, I just popped it down without thinking."

I rang the number and a nurse answered.

"How old is the child?" she asked.

"It's not a child," I told her. "It's my wife."

There was a silence on the phone. "I don't think I heard you," the nurse said.

"You heard me. My wife just took the dog's pill." I was humiliated. Concerned, too, but mostly humiliated. There was another silence while the nurse turned the pages of a book.

"I can't find anything," she said. "I don't think this has ever happened before."

"Probably not."

"I'll put you through to a doctor," said the nurse. And in a second the doctor was on the line.

"How much do they weigh?"

"Separately, or together?" I asked.

"Separately."

"One of them is about 100 or 105. The other's about 40 pounds."

"And your wife just took one tablet?"

"Right. She stopped herself at one."

"If you happen to have some ipecac around the house you might use that," the doctor said. "And I'd keep my eye on her for a rash or any trouble breathing. But I really don't think you have a problem."

"That's a relief," I said. "I hate to bother you, but I just wanted to be sure she wouldn't start barking or biting or something crazy like that."

"It's what we're here for," the doctor said.

I suppose now we'll have to begin watching for nips out of the house plants and locking the medicine cabinet again. But it's nice to be reminded the service is there when we need it, and is perfectly free.

95. *Corinne and Ben*

Summer approaches for them, this time, with not quite the same pure sense of exuberant release. There is wistfulness in it.

It isn't that they will mind school ending. School's socially useful, not generally unhealthy or apt to do too much lasting damage, but it's enslavement all the same. Any child who passed sadly into June, still yearning for more instruction, more examinations, would be ailing with something beyond the power of any book to cure.

No, they will be glad enough to have classes behind them. But the relief is mingled with regret. For, whereas earlier summers amounted to only a blessed interruption, after which all would go forward as before, this one will bring real change. Graduates will be going away from here by separate routes into the world. So lives and friendships are not an unbroken continuum. Things change. It is a lesson that experience will keep teaching in progressively more painful ways.

Many of these departing friends our daughters will miss keenly. And so will we—two of them especially, because we've known them best.

Corinne came as an exchange student from France, speaking that beautiful, maddeningly complex language which, on our best days, we struggle with so lamely. Other people were her American "parents," but we've had the luck to borrow her a time or two. In the winter she traveled with us to the mountains, slept in close quarters, set for us all a fine example of how to get down a ski hill with grace.

She is stylish and opinionated, both of which go with being French. There is about her the manner of someone who devours experience, ideas, argument, with fierce energy. She returns soon to the city of Rouen to start in the university. Rouen is where they burned the warrior saint, Joan of Arc. But no one had better trifle with our friend Corinne. She's equal parts sweetness and steel, and to know her at all is to be sure she'll find her way. Somewhere in this year she stole our hearts.

Our other young friend is Ben, who also speaks a language that, when he's excited or in a hurry, we cannot penetrate. It's the English of the New Zealanders.

Ben walks the world with luck, expecting the best, and no calamity will ever catch him. Sometimes he forgets his key, or otherwise gets locked out, but he knows there's a bed at our place. Or anyway a floor. Sometimes hunger overtakes him, and by happy chance there's a place at our table. As far as we're concerned, there always will be.

He runs the quarter-mile in 52 seconds. And plays Rugby, I'm told, like a demon. Above all, he enjoys fly-fishing for monster trout in the mountain waters of his homeland. As with Corinne, he's soon headed back for university. His real ambition is to play professional cricket. Maybe we should send a house key with him, so if his professors ever find that out, at least he'll have a place to crash.

Ben came one December day to help make Christmas cookies. Then, in an artless moment, dropped the whole first tray and turned them all to crumbs, but baked some more. He has shown us slides of New Zealand, of his parents, who look happy and incredibly young.

Those are the memories we'll keep. They are too few. And I suppose the realistic chances of our seeing these young friends again are not so good. But you balance the sadness of people leaving against the worse sadness of never having known them at all. That's the trade that life relentlessly imposes. And it is why summer, which is youth's time of sunny celebration, will begin this year under a shadow of regret.

Growing up is, most of all perhaps, the discovery of loss.

96. *Nature's Financial Aid*

In a matter of only months, now, the first daughter leaves for college, and the rabbits have come just in time. Providence is merciful. That's the only explanation I can give for the hares' sudden appearance and their amazing multiplication.

One day there was a single rabbit. No, there had to have been two. The next night, when we turned in the driveway, five of them crouched in the headlight beams of the car. There's no telling the number now. But they can be seen everywhere, at all hours of day and evening, nibbling in the flower bed, daintily clipping the grass. They are growing wonderfully fat.

The other afternoon, through an upstairs window, I spied two small boys venturing into the yard with BB guns. With a cry of dismay I thundered down the stairs and out the front door. *"Leave the protein alone!"* I barked at the trespassers. They seemed startled by my great agitation.

"We saw the rabbits, and we were just . . ."

"I know *exactly* what you were doing. Let me tell you. Someday you will grow up and find out what it costs to send a child to college. Then maybe you will have a little respect for other people's property."

"Yes, sir," they said. They were polite boys, but thoughtless.

"I don't mean to be unpleasant about it," I told them. "But I have just gotten the final tuition figures. When you look at those rabbits, probably you see the chance for a little sport. Right?"

"Yes, sir."

"Well, when I look at them, I see protein. There are squirrels living in the tree by the street. And chipmunks that use the garage. There's a pair of raccoons in the storm sewer, and we've attracted a nice flock of birds to the feeder. It's all protein. And *nothing—*"

I fixed them with a stern eye.

"Nothing is going to interfere with my family's survival. Do I make myself perfectly clear?"

"Yes, sir," they said again.

"All right, then. We have an understanding. The subject's closed. You can shoot out street lights, shoot out the windows of the house, throw rocks at the car. But leave the protein alone. If you frighten the rabbits and cause them to run off fat, you are taking food out of my family's mouth."

The boys left, and have not been back. But I continue to keep a close eye on the livestock, and also on the mailbox. Most of the winter was spent filling out financial aid forms, and now the reports from the colleges are coming in. Yesterday there was a letter from Pretentious U., one of those fancy schools in the East.

I ripped open the envelope and studied the analysis of our family's situation.

"What does it say?" my wife asked.

"It says we don't qualify. We're not rich and we're not poor. We have achieved what it calls *the tragic plateau of solvency.*"

"Is that all?"

"It suggests we supplement our diet with wild game."

"You fool! You mean you told them?"

"I had to. On the form it asked for a complete list of assets, and I was embarrassed to leave it blank. So I listed the rabbits."

And that may be what shot us down.

97. *Graduation*

Mothers do it regularly, but fathers are less experienced. I still can remember the panic, the raw terror, of that first time steering white-knuckled through the morning rush hour with eight little scholars—or was it *eighty?*—riding in a squealing knot in the rear of the station wagon.

The station wagon wore out. We got another, and it wore out, too, although the cost of education being what it is I still drive the thing.

The screams from the back subsided. In time, the tangle of small passengers resolved itself by gender. Some became little boys. Others turned into little girls. They drew apart, those two camps, and became solemn and suspicious.

All in a rush, then, they began arranging letters and numbers in ways that described and quantified the world. The ideas and the equations became more complicated. They made alliances, and conspired against us. For hours, sometimes, they would sit together, lost in secret talk. And these silences were at once blessed and ominous.

The years were divided neatly into the gift of summers and the tyranny of all the rest. And the summers were impossibly short. Cold nights and misty mornings by a northern lake. A cabin whose windows looked out on the furred flanks of mountains.

We didn't hold those things carefully enough. The time just got away.

Sorrows came to them. And some of those were griefs privately held, lodged in a new region of themselves we couldn't penetrate. Why do cats and dogs have to die? Why do people have to die? Why must friendships sometimes come apart? Why does everything always have to change? They needed answers we didn't have, because we, too, were oppressed by a growing sense of unreckonable loss.

I remember once—in this same time of year, as school drew to its end—sitting at a table outdoors and hearing the first sleepy sound of waking voices in the upstairs room, and wishing I had the power to stop time at exactly that sweet moment. Not stop it permanently, of course. Just for a while. And even before the wish was fully formed, the summer had passed, another year was lost.

They needed bicycles. Awkwardness gave way surprisingly to grace, and then to beauty. The utility of bicycles was superseded by the impossible dream of cars.

Strange it was to see them in shoes with slender heels. Impatient, they hesitated a moment to be photographed in the dress for the first dance. The photograph curls somewhere in a book.

Their rooms became alien principalities. Knock, please, and show your passport before entering.

Strangers appeared at the door. Not really strangers, because some of them were known from that earliest time, but little boys grown into almost-men, with changed voices and confident, self-contained eyes. And little girls, their childish faces recalled from car pool days, able now to take one's breath like a sudden body blow.

And all of them are outbound travelers, with mental baggage packed, like passengers on the quai, waiting for a ship. *Where are you going?* they ask one another. And answer with the names of places that seem, to the landbound, impossibly far away.

Ten minutes it takes to tell it.

Tomorrow evening they will stand together in caps and gowns to receive their certificates of passage. We who are assembled for the ceremony, in our confusion of pride and other feelings, will see their faces both as they are and as they were, across all the vanished years. And somehow, because convention requires it, I expect we will seem to smile.

98. *Women of Affairs*

It used to be their lazy season—a slow perambulation through a landscape of swimming pools, parks, ice cream shops and shaded yards where small friends played. The captivity of the classroom ended, they sank away into ease like queens of the Nile.

And I loved those years. No matter that I was prisoner in an office. Summer still brought a feeling of release. Such perfect freedom can be intoxicating, even if it isn't yours.

Now those hedonist daughters have become young women of affairs. One goes off to her work in the morning. The other has an evening job. They have gotten Social Security cards, established bank accounts, have things to do and places to go that have nothing to do with me. Sometimes our itineraries happen to cross. Their mother or I will come in from an errand just as they are outbound on one of theirs. With luck, there may be several minutes' overlap. Meals at which all four can sit at once have become a rarity. Occasionally, harried by the speeding clock, one or the other of them will skip eating altogether.

They never used to speak of being tired. Bed was something they went to only when commanded. Now, after a day of running, exhaustion fells them, and they give themselves up to a sleep too deep to be interrupted by any dream.

Thinking back, it seems to me that my own childhood lasted a good deal longer—straight on through the school years, and even some beyond. We lived in the shadow neither of *The Bomb* nor of the scramble for college places. There were more desks than there were students to fill them. If you thought you might want to attend, registrars were glad to have you. Patriotic service in the peacetime army was spent lounging on various Carolina beaches. Newspapering paid so poorly it couldn't reasonably be considered a vocation. So reporters became wonderfully skilled at a kind of basketball played with wadded paper and trash cans, and got irritable if some assignment interrupted their game.

All that has changed. Score poorly on the wrong test at age 17 and, ever afterward, in several hundred college admissions offices, you will be lumped with the dullards and deadbeats. Go in the military service and you risk getting hit by an anonymous bullet in an undeclared war over issues you don't understand in some place you can't pronounce.

Even journalism has taken on airs of social usefulness. Young reporters are hawk-eyed and ambitious. They write on computer screens instead of paper. You can't organize a game of throwing computers at wastebaskets without attracting the attention of the publisher. All the fun is gone.

I have been dragged kicking and protesting into the serious new world, and at a late age. My daughters are growing to it naturally. Sooner than I would have imagined it could happen, their lives are coming more and more to resemble this life I never willingly chose.

So summer mustn't be thought of anymore as a time for wasting. And there, precisely, is the intolerable loss.

99. *The Sudden Distance*

A young friend appeared, shaken, at our door. As she'd passed up the block in her car, a cat had darted from the curb and a wheel had struck it. It was hurt, she said—or maybe worse than hurt. And she'd come for help.

With selfish hearts, we first inventoried our own cats to be certain they all were indoors, then hurried out to the street to see what might be done. But there was no help to give.

We recognized the creature at the curb. It was the cat of our neighbors across the street. I bent to touch her, and saw how still she was, and the little dark stain spreading on the pavement. Except for that, you'd have thought she was only resting there. The blue eyes were not clouded, yet, by the sudden distance she had gone.

News like that you hate to carry, but there wasn't any choice. So we went in to telephone our neighbors and then out again to meet them at the curb.

Anyone who's shared enough lives to bear some griefs knows the drill. When the word comes, you accept immediately that it's true—that such things happen. Bill came out of the house already armed with a soft bath towel, Marjorie at his side. And even from a distance they knew she was, indeed, their old friend.

Her name was Inglenook, and she had a history, as do all the ones who share our roofs and chairs. She'd come to them from their daughter, when the daughter went away to live a while in Europe. So, in a way, she was a link to that earlier time in all their lives.

This they recalled in a few words, as we stood together looking sadly down.

"Are you sure she's—?" Marjorie asked. You know it, but hope is unreasonable.

"Yes," Bill said. Being a doctor, while it spares no pain, does teach a certain practicality. And he said: "They come as pets. But they leave as members of the family. I'll put her in the back yard, in our garden of the others."

Life's a process of subtraction, and when all is said no one ever saves anything. At least that is how it seems in the bitter moment. But memory is more powerful than loss. All the vanished creatures I have known come back to me now, on command, alive and young as they once were, more willingly than they ever came to any call or whistle.

The hard part is only at the first, and you have to manage it unaided.

Bill made a bundle in the towel. The wide blue eyes stared fixedly at the sky and trees, and the pale fur ruffled in the wind exactly as it had in life.

We all turned to leave, then. And as they started along the walk toward their house and the garden in the back, we heard them speak a last time the name of the friend they carried—by whose speaking they held back a moment longer the rush of thieving time.

C. W. Gusewelle

100. Reflected Light

There's no explaining such a day of autumn light in summer. A gift without reason, that's what it was.

Cool the morning began, the air blue, the pale sky cloudless. Presently the sun climbed above the trees and began its march toward afternoon. But, oddly, this day it was not a thing afire. Where it fell directly, there was only a pleasant warmth. And in every shadow was a sudden coolness.

That's how the light is in the high mountains. Or in the forest of the far north. Or in the shank of a fine October in the midlands, with the year in quick decline. But this was brutal summer, whose days are never kind. We'd driven to the country cabin, my daughters, the old dog and I, prepared to suffer some for being away together. And received, instead, the gift of that miracle day.

We did all the old things. Fished the pond, which sparkled with the rush of sudden little winds across it. Picked blackberries, crying out as the thorns caught us. Took aimless walks. Built fires for cooking over. Heard the red-winged blackbirds whistling from the reeds.

Listened to the unaccustomed stillness of our hearts.

The old dog, who at home can barely climb the stair, scampered like a pup. She swam twice across the pond, then, grinning, swam a river. And you could tell she was remembering how it was before the soreness came.

We remembered, too. Recalled the people—gone—whose shadows walk those woods. And remembered the day we began, together, the building of the tree house. We still think of the tree house as new, but the girls were small then, and now they're nearly grown. So something in our chronology is flawed.

224

In a few more weeks, the older of them will leave for college. The other remains another year, then follows off to somewhere in the world. The old dog's cataracts and deafness are worse. Some nights the leap to the bed defeats her. The changes start to be a load to carry.

How many more such country days? we thought, though no one asked it aloud.

Sometimes we just stopped, still as stones, to wonder at the peculiar quality of the light—shining on plump hay bales, on the curious cow faces across a fence, on weed stems. The trees at field's edge were drawn as in a painting, their shadows black.

Then evening came, and lakes of ground fog rose and pooled and flowed across the land. And in the darkness we drove nearly 50 miles to find ice cream to put the berries over, thus achieving the final perfection.

You're lucky if in a whole lifetime there are just a few days that fill you up that way. Nearly everything we did, we'd done before. But it was different this time. This time, besides the pleasure, there was about each moment a sense of conclusion—no, of *completion.*

The feeling had something to do with that strange summer day of autumn light, reflecting off leaf and water, reflecting off the memories of gathered years, in this season of all our uncertain passages.

Other books by The Westphalia Press

Bill Nunn's Column Book
"Teacher, Teacher, I Done It! I Done It! I Done Done It!"
Tom's Remembrance

These and Other Lands
The Painting Birds

QUICK AS SHADOWS PASSING

Photocomposed in Schoolbook type
by Modern Litho-Print Co.
Jefferson City, Missouri
1988